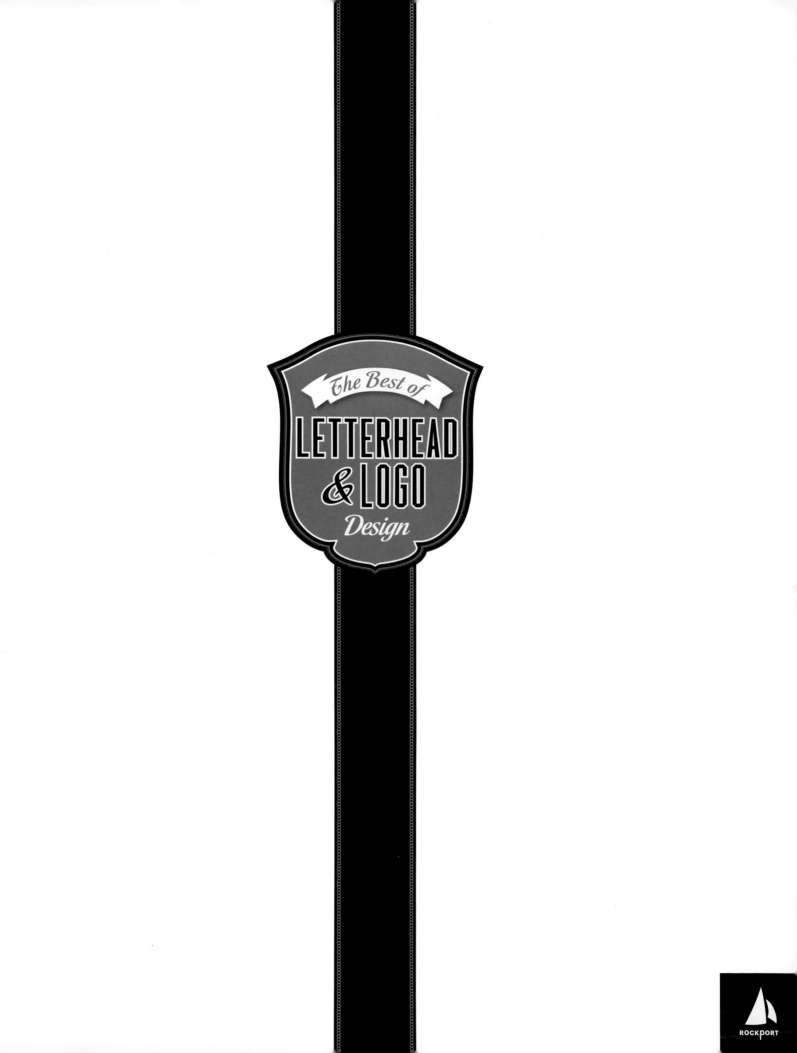

The Best of

LETTERHEAD & LOGO

Design

ROCKPORT

The Best of

LETTERHEAD & LOGO

Design

BEVERLY MASSACHUSETTS

ROCKPORT
PUBLISHERS

First published in the United States of America by
Rockport Publishers, a member of
Quayside Publishing Group
100 Cummings Center
Suite 406-L
Beverly, Massachusetts 01915-6101
Telephone: (978) 282-9590
Fax: (978) 283-2742
www.rockpub.com

ISBN-13: 978-1-59253-630-6
ISBN-10: 1-59253-630-1

10 9 8 7 6 5 4 3 2 1

Cover Image: insert photo credit
Cover Design: Rick Landers, LandersMiller
Edited by: Rachel Hewes and Allison Hodges

Printed in China

CONTENTS

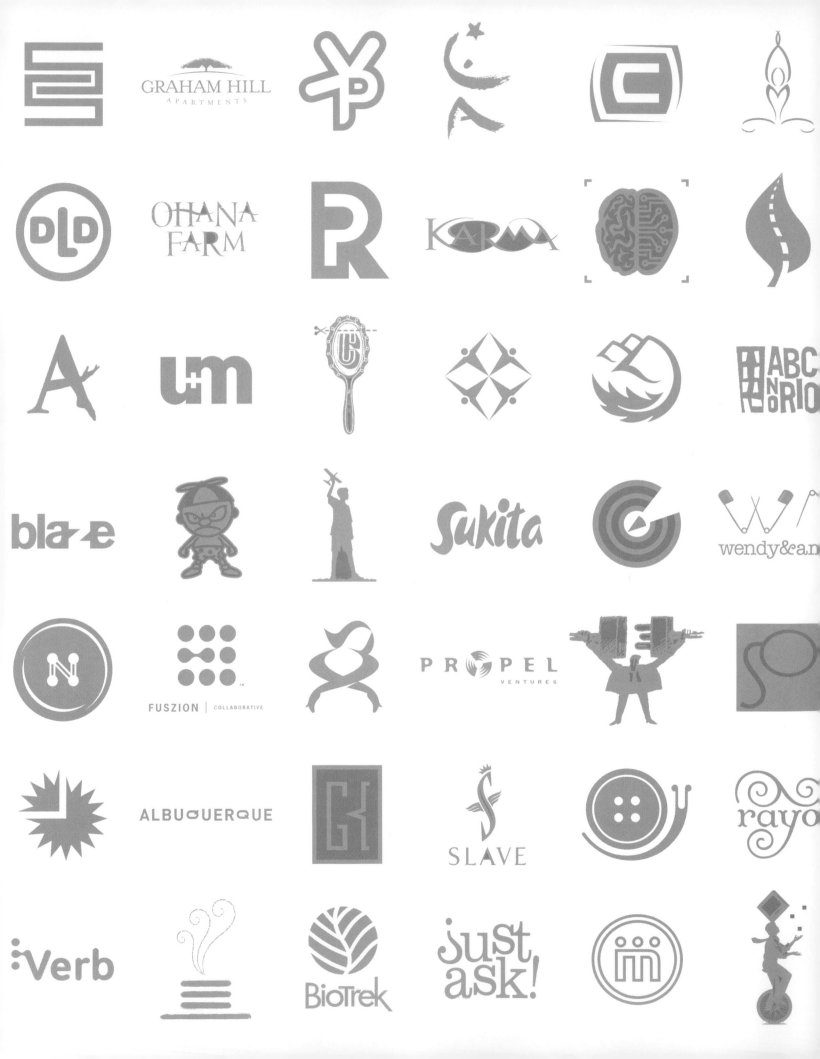

GRAHAM HILL
APARTMENTS

OHANA
FARM

ABC
N
O RIO

blaze

Sukita

wendy&can

PROPEL
VENTURES

FUSZION | COLLABORATIVE

ALBUQUERQUE

SLAVE

rayo

Verb

BioTrek

just
ask!

INTRODUCTION

The ability to grab, express, stimulate, push, provoke, blow. . .not really words you'd use to describe your corporate identity. But we think they describe some of the latest and most innovative letterhead and logo designs in use today. These designs grab attention, express a message, stimulate interest, push a product, provoke a response, and blow the competition out of the water!

Today's best designers are creating logo and letterhead designs that communicate their message with bold graphics, unexpected textures, brilliant colors, and special effects. Judicious use of these elements differentiates a good logo or letterhead system from a great one—and the truly great ones have the added ability to convey the clients' organizational personality at a glance.

The best way a logo or letterhead design can successfully communicate a company's message is with versatility. A good logo must be effective in one or multiple colors and able to appear in numerous sizes and in a variety of media. It may simultaneously need to be clear on a business card, huge on a billboard, and digital on a website.

The projects appearing in this book include fresh designs, striking illustrations, and clever executions. They are intended to inspire you to design logo and letterhead systems that creatively and effectively get the job done. Enjoy!

Chapter 1:

PROFESSIONAL SERVICES

SERVICE
860.659.8898

EMAIL
steepco@aol.com
steepco@juno.com

WWW
www.steep.com

ONE AND ONLY TEA MATCHBOX

PO BOX 89 ✳ SOUTH GLASTONBURY, CT ✳ 06073 USA

800 STEEPCO

steep

PREMIUM LEAF TEAS & HIGH-IMPACT COCOAS™

design firm	Plum Notion Design Laboratory
designers	Damion Silver, Jeff Piazza
client	Steep Tea

design firm	**Studio Hill**
art director	**Sandy Hill**
designers	**Sandy Hill, Emma Roberts-Wilson**
client	**Meyners + Co.**
tools	**Quark XPress, Macintosh**
paper/printing	**Strathmore Elements/ Black + Zhits Opaque White and Metallic Ink Temboss and Round Cornering**

design firm	Hornall Anderson Design Works, Inc.
art director	Jack Anderson
designers	Jack Anderson, Debra McCloskey, Holly Finlayson
client	Personify
tool	Macromedia FreeHand

design firm	Studio Hill
art director	Sandy Hill
designer	Emma Roberts-Wilson
client	Tech 2 Me
tools	Adobe Illustrator, Macintosh

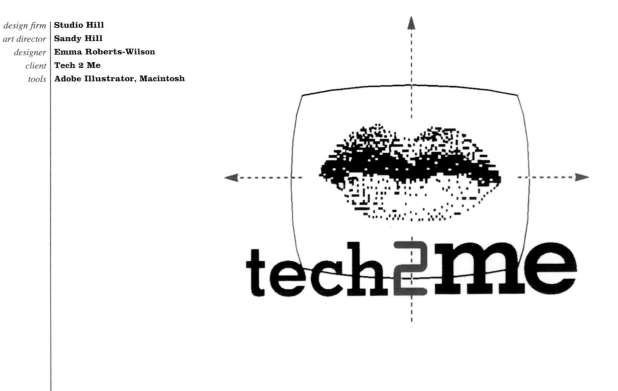

STRATEGIC CHANGE MANAGEMENT

4329 E. McDONALD   PHOENIX, AZ 85018   PH 602 840-6509   FAX 602 840-7501

design firm	**After Hours Creative**
art director	**After Hours Creative**
designer	**After Hours Creative**
client	**Strategic Change Management**

STRATEGIC CHANGE MANAGEMENT

SCOTT JACOBSON

4329 E. McDONALD   PHOENIX, AZ 85018
PH 602 840-6509   FAX 602 840-7501
ScottJ01@aol.com

STRATEGIC CHANGE MANAGEMENT
4329 EAST McDONALD
PHOENIX, AZ 85018

design firm | **Bob's Haus**
designer | **Bob Dahlquist**
client | **Bruce Whitelam, Whitelam + Whitelam**
tools | **Macromedia FreeHand 5.5, Macintosh Quadra 800**
paper/printing | **Classic Crest/Lithography**

14

design firm | **Bob's Haus**
designer | **Bob Dahlquist**
client | **Bruce Benning**
tools | **Macromedia FreeHand 5.5, Adobe Photoshop 4,**
 | **Macintosh G3**
paper/printing | **Classic Crest/Lithography**

innoVisions™

design firm	**Hornall Anderson Design Works, Inc.**
art director	**Jack Anderson**
designers	**Jack Anderson, Kathy Saito, Alan Copeland**
client	**Wells Fargo**
tool	**Macromedia FreeHand**

design firm	**Hornall Anderson Design Works, Inc.**
art director	**Jack Anderson**
designers	**Jack Anderson, Kathy Saito, Alan Copeland**
client	**Wells Fargo**
tool	**Macromedia FreeHand**
paper/printing	**70 lb. Mohawk Superfine, Bright White Text**

design firm	**Visual Dialogue**
art director	**Fritz Klaetke**
designer	**Fritz Klaetke**
client	**Kent Dayton**
tools	**Quark XPress, Adobe Photoshop, Macintosh Power PC**
paper/printing	**Mohawk/Shear Color Printing**

design firm	Vrontikis Design Office
art director	Petrula Vrontikis
designer	Logo and Stationary: Susan Carter
client	Levene, Neale, Bender and Rankin, L.L.P
tools	Adobe Illustrator, Quark XPress
paper/printing	Neenah Classic Crest/Coast Lithographics

design firm	Studio Bubblan
art director	Kari Palmquist
designers	Jeanette Palmquist, Kari Palmquist
client	MA Arkitekter
tools	Macromedia FreeHand, Quark XPress
paper/printing	Storafine/Etcetera Offset

JASNA

JANE AUSTEN SOCIETY
OF NORTH AMERICA

ELSA A. SOLENDER
President

BARBARA HELLERING
Vice President

GISELE RANKIN
Secretary

GEORGE BRANTZ
Treasurer

NILI OLAY
Assitant Treasurer

BARBARA LARKIN
*Membership Secretary-
United States*

NANCY THURSTON
*Membership Secretary-
Canada*

RENEE CHARRON
Treasurer-Canada

LEE RIDGEWAY
Publications Secretary

design firm	**Grafik Communications, Ltd.**
designers	**Kristin Moore, Richard Hamilton,**
	Judy Kirpich
client	**Jasna**
tools	**Quark XPress 3.3**

JASNA

JANE-AUSTEN SOCIETY
OF NORTH AMERICA

design firm	Vanderbyl Design
art director	Michael Vanderbyl
designers	Michael Vanderbyl, Amanda Fisher
client	Rocket Science
tools	Adobe Illustrator 7
paper/printing	Starwhite Vicksburg/Expressions litho

| design firm | Sayles Graphic Design |
| tool | Macintosh |

design firm | **Sayles Graphic Design**
art director | **John Sayles**
designer | **John Sayles**
client | **Big Daddy Photography**
tool | **Macintosh**
puper/printing | **Classic Crest Natural White/Offset**

design firm	**Vanderbyl Design**
art director	**Michael Vanderbyl**
designer	**Michael Vanderbyl**
client	**Archetype**
tool	**Quark XPress**
paper/printing	**Starwhite Vicksburg/Archetype**

design firm	Walker Thomas Associates Melbourne
art director	Peter Walker
designers	Catherine Thomas, Neil Stockwell
client	Walker Thomas/Walker Pinfold Associates
tools	Quark XPress, Adobe Photoshop
paper/printing	Dalton Clipper Corporate/Four-color lithography

Walker Pinfold Associates

wpa
LONDON

Walker Thomas Associates

Catherine Thomas
Design Director

Walker Thomas Associates
Melbourne Pty Ltd
Design Consultants

Top Floor, Osment Building
Maples Lane, Prahran
Victoria 3181 Australia
T 03 9521 4433
F 03 9521 4466
E wta@creativeaccess.com.au

Walker Pinfold Associates

with compliments

Associated Office

Walker Pinfold Associates
London Limited
Design Consultants

17 The Ivories
6 Northampton Street
London N1 2HY

Walker Thomas Associates
Melbourne Pty Ltd
Design Consultants

Top Floor, Osment Building
Maples Lane, Prahran
Victoria 3181

T 0171 354 5887
F 0171 354 0319
E wpalondon@aapi.co.uk

T 03 9521 4433
F 03 9521 4466
E wta@creativeaccess.com.au

Walker Pinfold Associates
London Limited
Design Consultants

17 The Ivories
6 Northampton Street
London N1 2HY

T 0171 354 5887
F 0171 354 0319
E wpalondon@aapi.co.uk

Reg. in England No: 238 4906

Associated Office

Walker Thomas Associates
Melbourne Pty Ltd
Design Consultants

Top Floor, Osment Building
Maples Lane, Prahran
Victoria 3181

T 03 9521 4433
F 03 9521 4466
E wta@creativeaccess.com.au

A.C.N. 066 086 888

design firm	**After Hours Creative**
art director	**After Hours Creative**
designer	**After Hours Creative**
client	**enx**

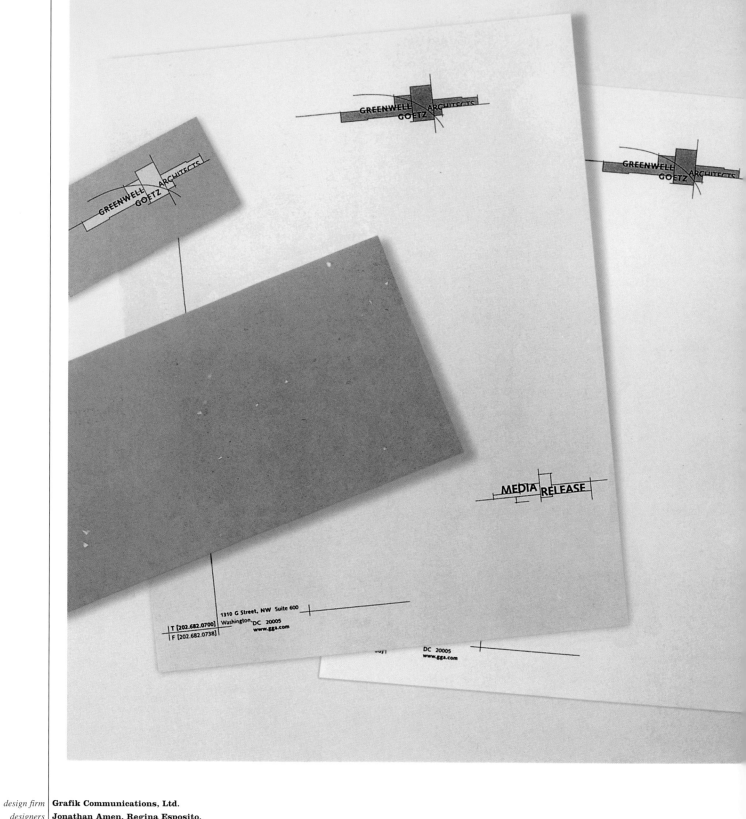

design firm	**Grafik Communications, Ltd.**
designers	**Jonathan Amen, Regina Esposito,**
	Gregg Glaviano, Judy Kirpich
client	**Greenwell Goetz Architects**
tools	**Macromedia FreeHand, Quark XPress**
paper/printing	**French Frostone Frostbite and Tundra,**
	Gilbert Neutech

design firm	Modelhart Grafik-Design DA
art director	Herbert O. Modelhart
designer	Herbert O. Modelhart
client	Optik Mayr
tools	Quark XPress, Adobe Illustrator, Adobe Photoshop
paper/printing	Olin/Two-color, Business Card Cellophane

design firm	**Henderson Tyner Art Co.**
art director	**Troy Tyner**
designers	**Troy Tyner, Amanda Love**
client	**Place Photography**
tool	**Macromedia FreeHand**
paper/printing	**Strathmore Writing/Dicksons Printing Co.**

design firm	**Woodworth Associates**
art director	**Brad Woodworth**
designer	**Steve Westfal**
client	**Landmark Builders**
tools	**Adobe Pagemaker, Macromedia FreeHand**
paper/printing	**Strathmore Writing/Offset**

design firm	**Karacters Design Group**
creative director	**Maria Kennedy**
designer	**Matthew Clark**
client	**Rick Etkin Photography**
tools	**Adobe Illustrator, Macintosh**
paper/printing	**Confetti/Broadway Printers**

design firm	**Insight Design Communications**
art directors	**Tracy Holdeman, Sherrie Holdeman**
designers	**Tracy Holdeman, Sherrie Holdeman**
client	**Rock Island Studios, Inc.**
tools	**Adobe Photoshop, Macromedia FreeHand, Macintosh**

VECTOR XXI,
Estudos de
Desenvolvimento
Económico e Social, Lda.

Av. Central, 45
Tel. 053. 616906/510
Fax 053. 611872
4710 Braga
Portugal

design firm	**Vestígio, Lda.**
art director	**Emanuel Barbosa**
designer	**Emanuel Barbosa**
client	**Vector XXI**
tools	**Macromedia FreeHand, Adobe Photoshop, Macintosh**

design firm	**Nesnadny + Schwartz**
designers	**Mark Schwartz, Joyce Nesnadny**
client	**Fortran Printing, Inc.**
tools	**Quark XPress, Adobe Illustrator, Adobe Photoshop**
paper/printing	**70 lb. Champion Benefit Cream/Fortran Printing, Inc.**

design firm	**Warren Group**
art director	**Linda Warren**
designer	**Annette Hanzer Pfau**
client	**client Candace Pearson**
tools	**tools Quark XPress, Adobe Illustrator**
paper/printing	**Strathmore Writing/Barbara's Place**

(candace P E A R S O N) THE WRITERS' PROJECT | 2016 Valentine Street Los Angeles, CA 90026

213.665-0615 telephone | 213.665-0990 facsimile

cp813@westworld.com

¹Halley's Comet.

²Indy 500. (THINGS THAT M O V E)

³San Andreas Fault.

⁴Candace Pearson.

CANDACE PEARSON IS PLEASED TO ANNOUNCE
she has moved to new offices.

Same phone numbers. Same great copywriting.

ADS. ANNUALS. COLLATERAL. DIRECT MAIL. PACKAGING. PRODUCT NAMING. WEB WORK.

(candace P E A R S O N)

213.665-0615 telephone

THE WRITERS' PROJECT

[A] MODERN

2016 Valentine Street | 213.665-0990 facsimile
Los Angeles, CA 90026 | cp813@westworld.com

(DEVELOPMENT OF MAJUSCULE)
FIRST LETTER OF THE ENGLISH ALPHABET
developed from Greek Alpha.

[K A A A]
SEMITIC GREEK ETRUSCAN LATIN MODERN

(candace P E A R S O N) | THE WRITERS' PROJECT
2016 Valentine Street
Los Angeles, CA 90026

[A] MODERN

(candace P E A R S O N)

THE WRITERS' PROJECT
2016 Valentine Street Los Angeles, CA 90026

Law Offices of
LANCE A. LICHTER

TEL
414 375-6868

FAX
414 375-6869

W62 N551 Washington Avenue Cedarburg, Wisconsin 53012

design firm	**Becker Design**
art director	**Neil Becker**
designer	**Neil Becker**
client	**Lance A. Lichter**
tool	**Quark XPress**

Law Offices of
LANCE A. LICHTER

TEL
414 375-6868

FAX
414 375-6869

W62 N551
Washington Avenue Cedarburg, Wisconsin
53012

Law Offices of
LANCE A. LICHTER

W62 N551 Washington Avenue Cedarburg, Wisconsin 53012

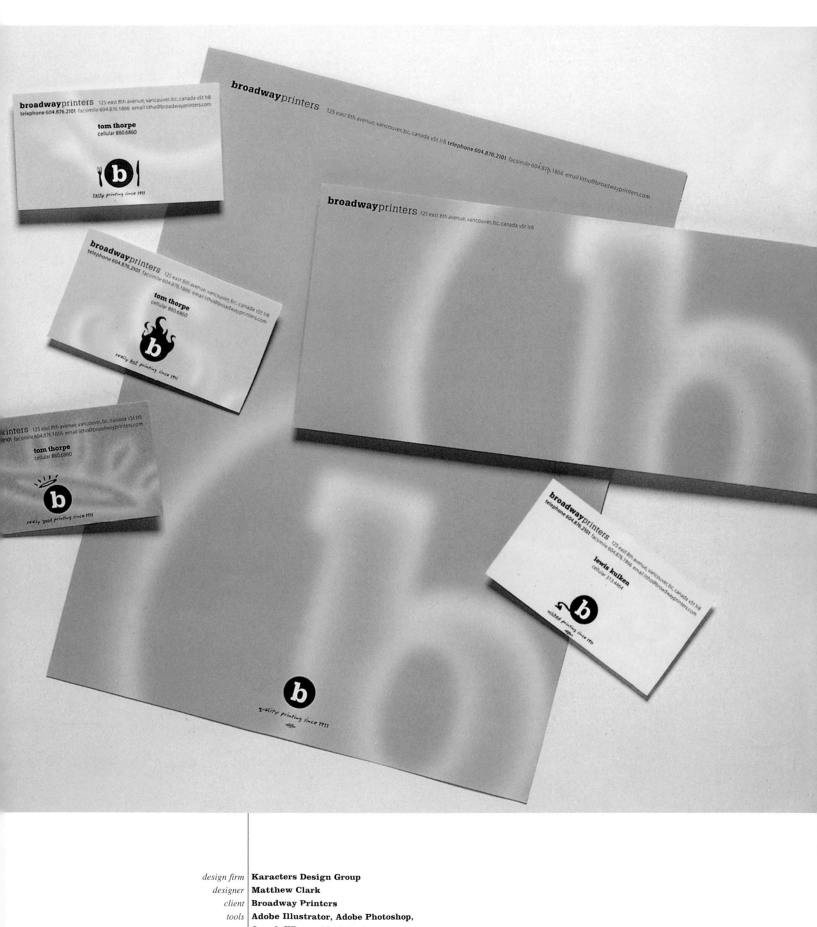

design firm | **Karacters Design Group**
designer | **Matthew Clark**
client | **Broadway Printers**
tools | **Adobe Illustrator, Adobe Photoshop,**
| **Quark XPress, Macintosh**
paper/printing | **Starwhite Vicksburg/Broadway Printers**

design firm	Spin Productions
art directors	Dale Smith, Kathi Prosser
designers	Dale Smith, Kathi Prosser
client	Spin Productions
tools	Adobe Illustrator, Adobe Photoshop
paper/printing	Plainfield Pinweave/CJ Graphics

design firm | **Greteman Group**
art directors | **Sonia Greteman, James Strange**
designer | **James Strange**
client | **R. Messner**
tools | **Macromedia FreeHand, Macintosh**

design firm | **Barbara Chan Design**
art director | **Barbara Chan**
designer | **Barbara Chan**
client | **Husband & Associates**
tools | **Adobe Illustrator 7.0, Macintosh G3**

design firm | **Russell, Inc.**
art director | **Laura Wills**
designer | **Laura Wills**
client | **Certicom, Inc.**

design firm	**After Hours Creative**
art director	**After Hours Creative**
designer	**After Hours Creative**
client	**Second Opinion**

design firm | **Siebert Design**
art director | **Lori Siebert**
designer | **Scott Hull Associates**
client | **Arnold Printing**

TMG classic mini radios

design firm | **Jim Lange Design**
art director | **Genji Leclair**
designer | **Jim Lange**
client | **TMG**
tool | **Macintosh**

design firm | **Synergy Design**
art director | **Leon Alvarado**
designer | **Leon Alvarado**
client | **The Room**
tools | **Macromedia FreeHand, Macintosh**
paper/printing | **Vinyl/Silk screening**

design firm | **Choplogic**
art directors | **Walter McCord, Mary Cawein**
designers | **Walter McCord, Mary Cawein**
client | **Internet Tool & Die**
tools | **Adobe Ilustrator, Quark XPress**
paper/printing | **Fox River, Simpson Starwhite Vicksburg/**
| **Two-color lithography**

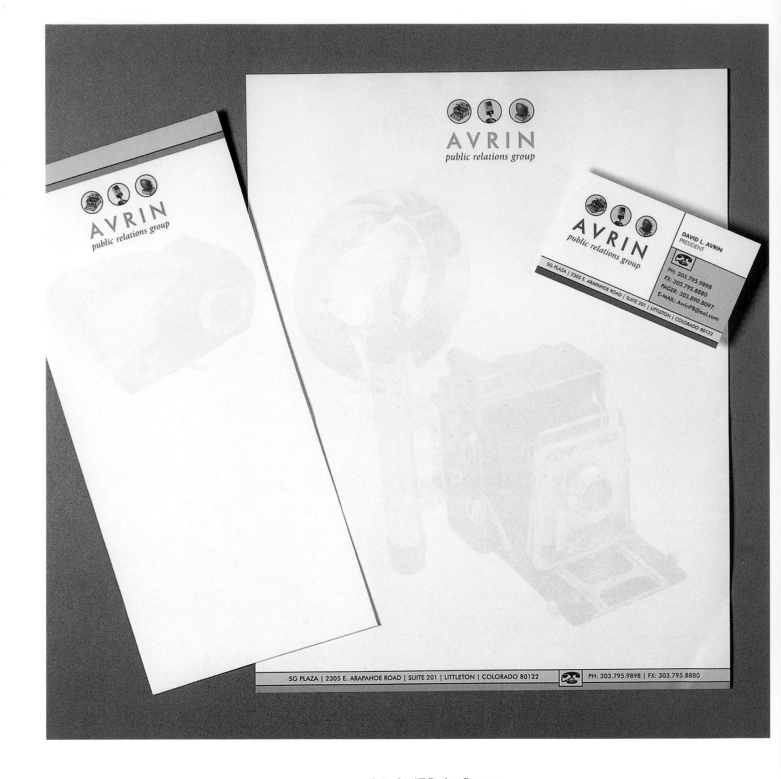

design firm | **X Design Company**
art director | **Alex Valderrama**
designer | **Alex Valderrama**
client | **Avrin Public Relations**

PROCESS SOLUTIONS

NEAL G. ANDERSON, PH.D.

129 UPPER CREEK ROAD, STOCKTON, NJ 08559
PHONE: (908) 996-2585, FAX: (908) 996-6505
E-MAIL: ANDERSON@ECLIPSE.NET

design firm	**Howard Levy Design**
art director	**Howard Levy**
designer	**Howard Levy**
client	**Process Solutions**

PROCESS SOLUTIONS

129 UPPER CREEK ROAD, STOCKTON, NJ 08559
PHONE: (908) 996-2585, FAX: (908) 996-6505
E-MAIL: ANDERSON@ECLIPSE.NET

design firm	**Plum Notion Design Laboratory**
art director	**Damion Silver**
designer	**Damion Silver**
client	**Bikers Edge Bike Shop**
tools	**Adobe Illustrator, Adobe Photoshop**

design firm	**Han/Davis Group**
art director	**Ed Han**
designer	**Ed Han**
client	**Inform Research & Marketing**
tool	**Adobe Illustrator**

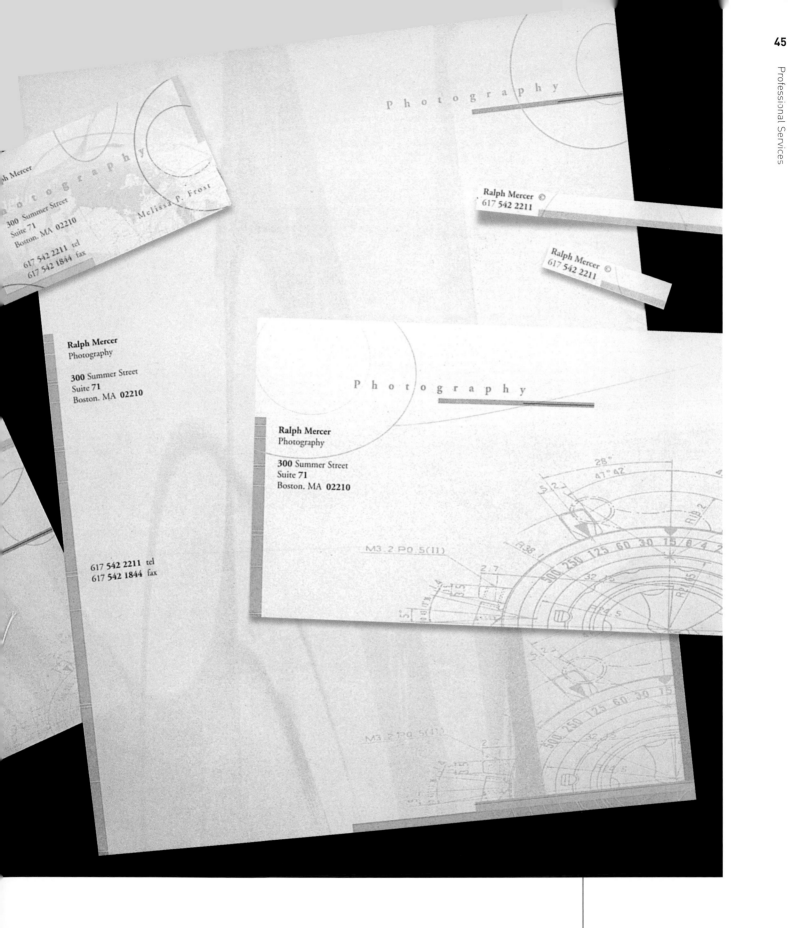

design firm	**Laughlin/Winkler, Inc.**
art directors	**Mark Laughlin, Ellen Winkler**
designer	**Ellen Winkler**
client	**Ralph Mercer Photography**
tools	**Quark XPress, Macintosh G3**
paper/printing	**Mohawk/Alpha Press**

design firm	**Design Guys**
art director	**Steven Sikora**
designer	**Amy Kirkpatrick**
client	**Mike Rabe Music Engraving**
tool	**Adobe Illustrator**
paper/printing	**Gray Fine Art Paper, Beckett Concept**
	Sand Text, Curtis Black Vellum
	Cover/Offset, Park Printing, Exceptional
	Engraving (Card)

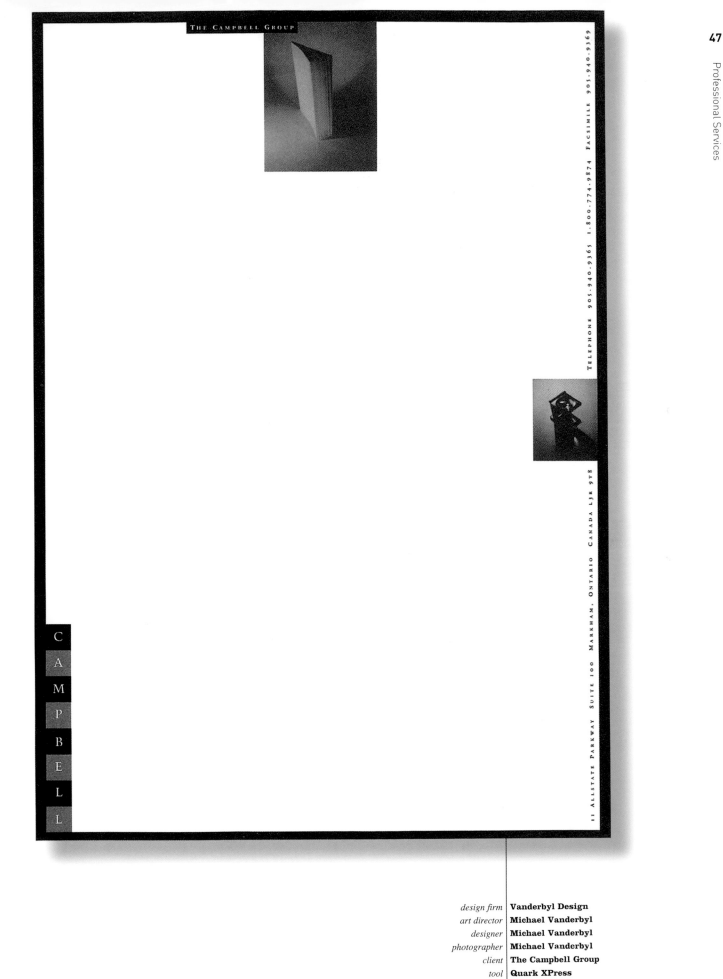

THE CAMPBELL GROUP

TELEPHONE 905.940.9365 1.800.774.9874 FACSIMILE 905.940.9369

11 ALLSTATE PARKWAY SUITE 100 MARKHAM, ONTARIO CANADA L3R 9T8

C
A
M
P
B
E
L
L

design firm	**Vanderbyl Design**
art director	**Michael Vanderbyl**
designer	**Michael Vanderbyl**
photographer	**Michael Vanderbyl**
client	**The Campbell Group**
tool	**Quark XPress**
paper/printing	**Starwhite Vicksburg-The Campbell Group**

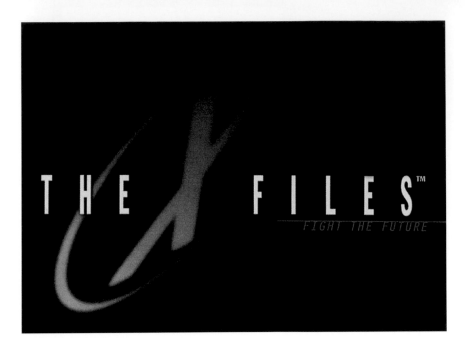

design firm | **Hamagami/Carroll & Associates**
art director | **Justin Carroll**
designer | **Tony Mauro**
client | **Twentieth-Century Fox**

design firm | **Hamagami/Carroll & Associates**
art director | **Justin Carroll**
designer | **Tony Mauro**
client | **Twentieth-Century Fox**

DESIGN FIRM	A1 Design
DESIGNER	Amy Gregg
CLIENT	Sandglass
TOOLS	Adobe Illustrator, Macintosh

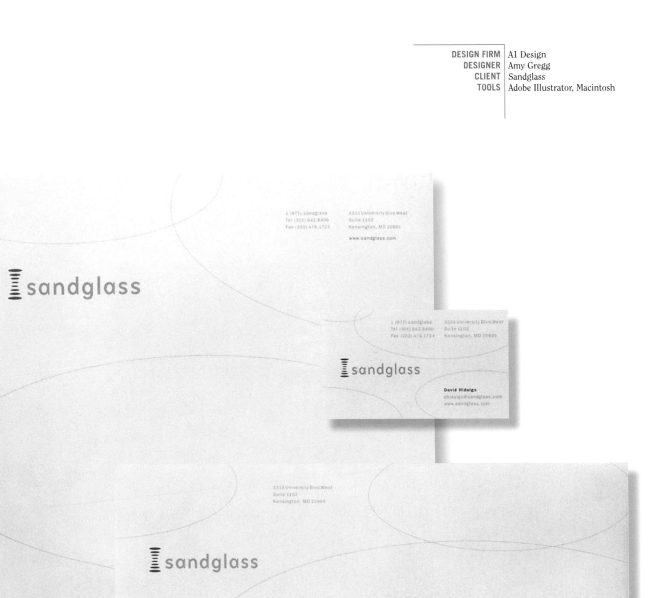

DESIGN FIRM	A1 Design
DESIGNER	Amy Gregg
CLIENT	Red Whistle
TOOLS	Adobe Illustrator, Macintosh

DESIGN FIRM	Buchanan Design
ART DIRECTOR	Bobby Buchanan
DESIGNER	Bobby Buchanan
CLIENT	Davinci by Design
TOOLS	Adobe Illustrator, Macintosh

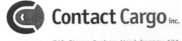

DESIGN FIRM	Beaulien Concepts Graphiques, Inc.
ART DIRECTOR	Gilles Beaulien
DESIGNER	Gilles Beaulien
CLIENT	Contact Cargo
TOOLS	Adobe Illustrator, Macintosh

DESIGN FIRM	Christopher Gorz Design
ART DIRECTOR	Chris Gorz
DESIGNER	Chris Gorz
CLIENT	Scubalogy
TOOLS	Adobe Illustrator, Macintosh

Basic, Advanced & Specialty SCUBA Instruction

DESIGN FIRM	Christopher Gorz Design
ART DIRECTOR	Chris Gorz
DESIGNER	Chris Gorz
CLIENT	EnvestNet
TOOLS	Adobe Illustrator, Macintosh

DESIGN FIRM | Design Center
ART DIRECTOR | John Reger
DESIGNER | Sherwin Schwartzrock
CLIENT | Market Trust
TOOLS | Macromedia FreeHand, Macintosh

MARKETTRUST

DESIGN FIRM | D4 Creative Group
ART DIRECTOR | Wicky W. Lee
DESIGNER | Wicky W. Lee
CLIENT | Ajunto
TOOLS | Adobe Illustrator, Quark XPress, Macintosh G4

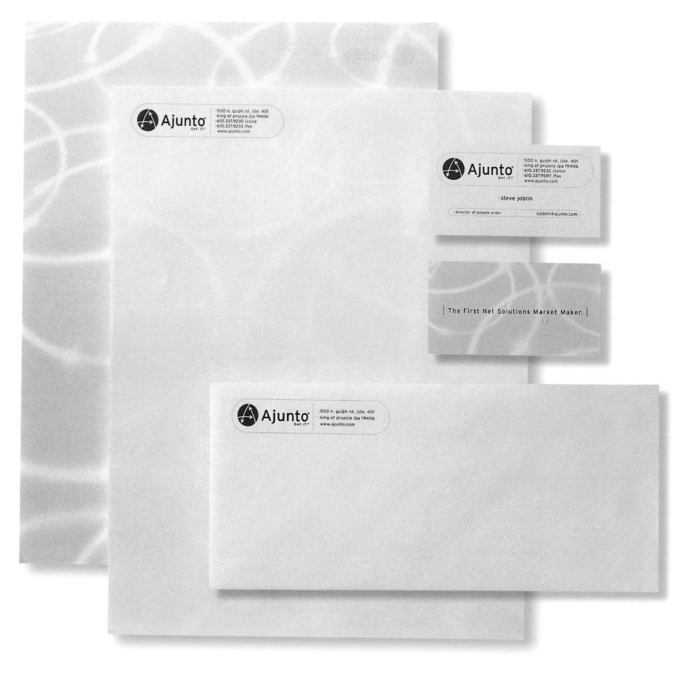

DESIGN FIRM | DogStar
ART DIRECTOR | Clyde Goode/HSR Business to Business
DESIGNER | Rodney Davidson
CLIENT | spotlightsolutions.com
TOOL | Macromedia FreeHand 7

DESIGN FIRM | DogStar
ART DIRECTOR | Mike Rapp/Gear
DESIGNER | Rodney Davidson
CLIENT | Waterbrook Press (Fisherman Bible Study Series)
TOOL | Macromedia FreeHand 7

DESIGN FIRM	Fuel Creative
ART DIRECTOR	Eric B. Whitlock
DESIGNER	Eric B. Whitlock
CLIENT	Think Floors
TOOL	Adobe Illustrator

CASTILE
VENTURES

DESIGN FIRM	Gee + Chung Design
ART DIRECTOR	Earl Gee
DESIGNER	Earl Gee
CLIENT	Castile Ventures
TOOLS	Adobe Illustrator, Quark XPress

PARTECH

INTERNATIONAL

DESIGN FIRM	Gee + Chung Design
ART DIRECTORS	Earl Gee, Fani Chung
DESIGNERS	Earl Gee, Fani Chung
CLIENT	Partech International
TOOLS	Adobe Illustrator, Quark Xpress

DESIGN FIRM	Gee + Chung Design
ART DIRECTOR	Earl Gee
DESIGNERS	Earl Gee, Kay Wu
CLIENT	Netigy Corporation
TOOLS	Adobe Illustrator, Quark Xpress

Netigy^{SM}

DESIGN FIRM | Graphiculture
ART DIRECTOR | Beth Mueller
DESIGNER | Beth Mueller
CLIENT | Targert Corporation
TOOL | Quark XPress

DESIGN FIRM | Gardner Design
ART DIRECTOR | Bill Gardner
DESIGNER | Bill Gardner
CLIENT | Buzz Cuts Maximum Lawncare
TOOL | Macromedia FreeHand

DESIGN FIRM	Hornall Anderson Design Works, Inc.
ART DIRECTOR	Jack Anderson
DESIGNERS	Kathy Saito, Gretchen Cook, James Tee, Julie Lock, Henry Yiu, Alan Copeland, Sonja Max
CLIENT	Gettuit.com
TOOL	Macromedia FreeHand

gettuit.com™

DESIGN FIRM	Hornall Anderson Design Works, Inc.
ART DIRECTORS	Jack Anderson, Debra McCloskey
DESIGNERS	Jack Anderson, Debra McCloskey, John Anderle, Andrew Wicklund
CLIENT	Truck Bay
TOOL	Adobe Illustrator

DESIGN FIRM	Hornall Anderson Design Works, Inc.
ART DIRECTOR	Jack Anderson
DESIGNERS	Jack Anderson, Katha Dalton, Gretchen Cook, Alan Florsheim, Andrew Smith, Ed Lee
CLIENT	epods
TOOLS	Macromedia FreeHand, Adobe Illustrator

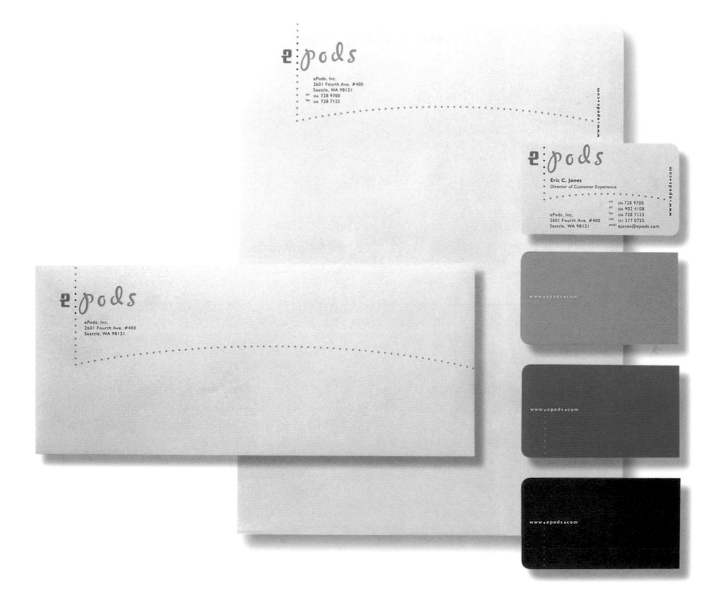

DESIGN FIRM	Hornall Anderson Design Works, Inc.
ART DIRECTOR	Jack Anderson
DESIGNERS	Jack Anderson, Bruce Stigler, James Tee, Henry Yiu
CLIENT	Javelin
TOOL	Macromedia FreeHand

DESIGN FIRM	Insight Design Communications
ART DIRECTORS	Sherrie & Tracy Holdeman
DESIGNERS	Sherrie & Tracy Holdeman
CLIENT	ironweed strategy
TOOL	Macromedia FreeHand 9.0.1

DESIGN FIRM	Insight Design Communications
ART DIRECTORS	Sherrie & Tracy Holdeman
DESIGNERS	Sherrie & Tracy Holdeman
CLIENT	CallSmart
TOOLS	Macromedia FreeHand 9.0.1

DESIGN FIRM	Insight Design Communications
ART DIRECTORS	Sherrie & Tracy Holdeman
DESIGNERS	Sherrie & Tracy Holdeman
CLIENT	Face to Face
TOOL	Hand Drawn, Macromedia FreeHand 9.0.1

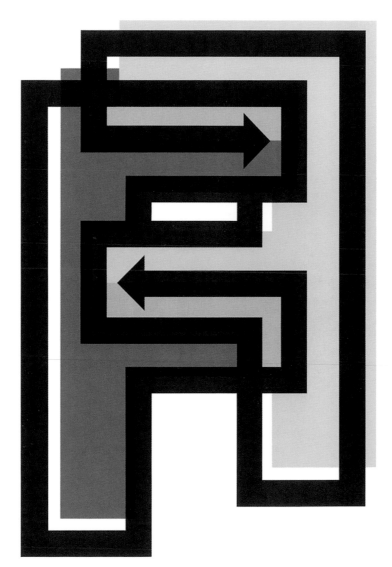

DESIGN FIRM | I. Paris Design
ART DIRECTOR | Isaac Paris
DESIGNER | Isaac Paris
CLIENT | TOKYO Wireless
TOOL | Adobe Illustrator 8

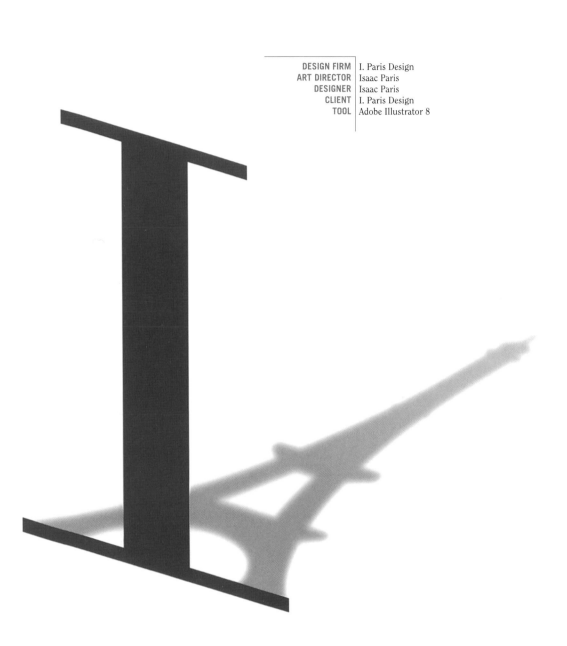

DESIGN FIRM	I. Paris Design
ART DIRECTOR	Isaac Paris
DESIGNER	Isaac Paris
CLIENT	I. Paris Design
TOOL	Adobe Illustrator 8

DESIGN FIRM	Jay Smith Design
ART DIRECTOR	Jay Smith
DESIGNER	Jay Smith
CLIENT	3 Guys and a Mower
TOOLS	Adobe Illustrator, Macintosh

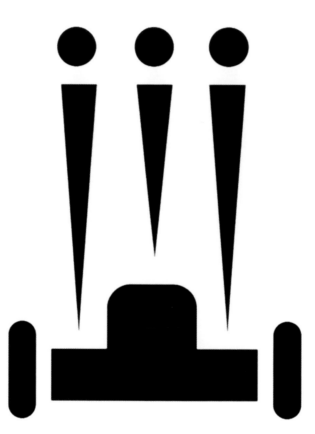

DESIGN FIRM	Energy Energy Design
ART DIRECTOR	Leslie Guidice
DESIGNER	Jeanette Aramburu
CLIENT	Mucho.com
TOOLS	Adobe Illustrator, Macintosh

DESIGN FIRM	Energy Energy Design
ART DIRECTOR	Leslie Guidice
SENIOR DESIGNERS	Stacy Guidice, Jeanette Aramburu
CLIENT	StaffBridge
TOOLS	Adobe Illustrator, Macintosh

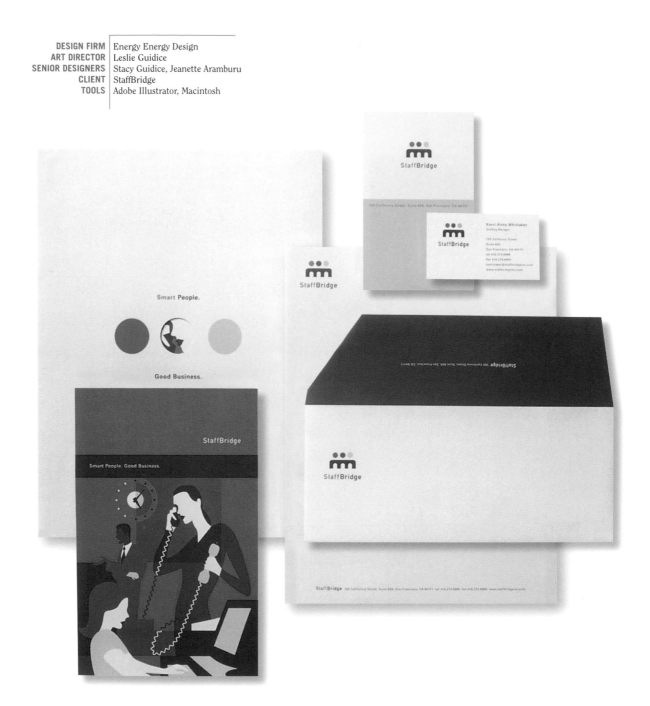

DESIGN FIRM	R2 Design/Ramalho & Rebelo, Lda.
ART DIRECTORS	Liza Ramalho, Artur Rebelo
DESIGNERS	Liza Ramalho, Artur Rebelo
CLIENT	West Coast
TOOL	Macromedia FreeHand

DESIGN FIRM	Refinery Design Company
ART DIRECTOR	Michael Schmalz
DESIGNER	Michael Schmalz
CLIENT	Historical Development Leasing Corporation
TOOLS	Macromedia FreeHand, Macintosh

i-connect

DESIGN FIRM	The Riordon Design Group
ART DIRECTORS	Ric Riordon, Dan Wheaton
DESIGNER	Alan Krpan
CLIENT	Ford Motor Company/Canada
TOOL	Adobe Illustrator

DESIGN FIRM	Sayles Graphic Design
ART DIRECTOR	John Sayles
DESIGNER	John Sayles
CLIENT	Car Hop
TOOLS	Adobe Illustrator, Macintosh

DESIGN FIRM	Sayles Graphic Design
ART DIRECTOR	John Sayles
DESIGNER	John Sayles
CLIENT	McArthur Company
TOOLS	Adobe Illustrator, Macintosh

DESIGN FIRM	Sayles Graphic Design
ART DIRECTOR	John Sayles
DESIGNER	John Sayles
CLIENT	Kelling Management Group
TOOLS	Adobe Illustrator, Macintosh

HYBRID

70 Federal Street
Boston Massachusetts
02110

Telephone
617 728 · 4442

Telefax
617 728 · 4448

NASSAR DESIGN | ART DIRECTOR **NÉLIDA NASSAR** | DESIGNER **MARGARITA ENCOMIENDA** | CLIENT **HYBRID**

PLATFORM CREATIVE | ART DIRECTOR ROBERT DIETZ | DESIGNER RENEE YANCY | CLIENT STRIKEPLATE, TYLER CARTIER

A2-GRAPHICS/SW/HK | ART DIRECTORS SCOTT WILLIAMS, HENRIK KUBEL | CLIENT **1508**

1

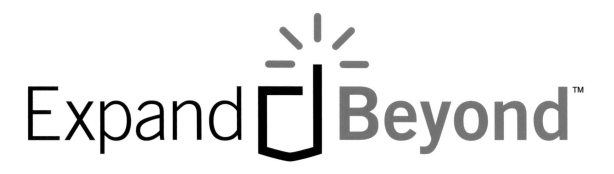

2

3

4

1 **LISKA + ASSOCIATES** | ART DIRECTOR **STEVE LISKA** | DESIGNERS **RUDI BACKART, STEVE LISKA** | CLIENT **EXPAND BEYOND**

2 **I. PARIS DESIGN** | ART DIRECTOR **ISAAC PARIS** | CLIENT **CITY PLUMBING, INC.**

3 **SAYLES GRAPHIC DESIGN** | ART DIRECTOR **JOHN SAYLES** | CLIENT **CATCH SOME RAYZ**

4 **GOTTSCHALK + ASH INTERNATIONAL** | ART DIRECTOR **STUART ASH** | DESIGNER **SONIA CHOW** | CLIENT **HATCH DESIGN INC.**

thinkdesign
and communications

John Wehmann
john@thinkdesign.net

thinkdesign
and communications

407 N. Washington Street   Suite 102   Falls Church, VA 22046
tel: 703.237.0045   **fax:** 703.237.7538   **web:** www.thinkdesign.net

thinkdesign
and communications
407 North Washington Street, Suite 102
Falls Church, VA 22046

407 North Washington Street   Suite 102   Falls Church, Virginia 22046   tel: 703.237.0045   fax: 703.237.7538   web: www.thinkdesign.net

THINKDESIGN & COMMUNICATIONS | ART DIRECTOR **JIM GARZIONE** | DESIGNERS **JOHN WEHMANN, KRISTEN ULLRICH** | CLIENT **THINKDESIGN**

MONDERER DESIGN

2067 Massachusetts Avenue
Cambridge, MA 02140-1337

617 661 6125 FAX 661 6126
www.monderer.com

> Design + Visual Communications

RED DESIGN | ART DIRECTORS ED TEMPLETON, HAMISH MAKGIU | DESIGNER RED DESIGN | CLIENT RED DESIGN

BALANCE DESIGN | ART DIRECTOR **CAREY JONES** | CLIENT **BALANCE DESIGN**

RUBIN CORDARO DESIGN | ART DIRECTOR BRUCE RUBIN | DESIGNER JIM CORDARO | CLIENT RUBIN CORDARO DESIGN

odelldesigngroup
723 broadway avenue east
seattle washington 98102

odelldesigngroup

jack k. odell, AIA

723 broadway avenue east
seattle washington 98102

78-7092 heeia way
kailua-kona hawaii 96740

t 206.329.4338
f 206.860.0045
c 206.953.2509
jodell@odelldesign.com

t 206.329.4338
f 206.860.0045

723 broadway avenue east
seattle washington 98102

MONSTER DESIGN | ART DIRECTORS **HANNAH WYGAL, THERESA VERANTH** | DESIGNER **HANNAH WYGAL** | CLIENT **ODELL DESIGN GROUP**

BURD & PATTERSON | ART DIRECTORS TRENTON BURD, BRIAN PATTERSON | DESIGNER TRENTON BURD | CLIENT BURD & PATTERSON

Martin Maretzki, RHU
axiz@sympatico.ca

t 905 521 2817   f 905 521 2838
100 King St. W., Suite 1400
Hamilton, ON L8P 1A2

ax/iz financial solutions
strategic - unique - proven

t 905 521 2817   f 905 521 2838
100 King St. W., Suite 1400
Hamilton, ON L8P 1A2

THE RIORDON DESIGN GROUP | DESIGNER **AMY MONTGOMERY** | CLIENT **AX/IZ FINANCIAL SOLUTIONS** | ART DIRECTOR **DAN WHEATON**

1

FRESHBRAND

2

3

4

PARADIGM

PUBLISHING GROUP

the
ESPRESSO
GOURMET

1 **FRESHBRAND, INC.** | ART DIRECTOR **MARCEL VENTER** | CLIENT **FRESHBRAND**

2 **YES DESIGN** | ART DIRECTOR **YVONNE SAKOWSKI** | CLIENT **REZAW-PLAST**

3 **GASKET** | ART DIRECTOR **MIKE CHRISTOFFEL** | DESIGNERS **MIKE CHRISTOFFEL, TODD HANSSON** | CLIENT **FIONA TUCKER**

4 **MORRIS CREATIVE INC.** | ART DIRECTOR **STEVEN MORRIS** | CLIENT **ESPRESSO GOURMET**

1

2

3

4

1 LOVE COMMUNICATIONS | ART DIRECTOR PRESTON WOOD | DESIGNERS CRAIG LEE, PRESTON WOOD | CLIENT CRAIG LEE

2 UP DESIGN BUREAU | ART DIRECTOR TRAVIS BROWN | CLIENT CHRISTY PETERS

3 IRIDIUM, A DESIGN AGENCY | ART DIRECTOR MARIO L'ECUYER | CLIENT NEXWAVE CORPORATION

4 CATO PURNELL PARTNERS | ART DIRECTOR CATO PURNELL PARTNERS | CLIENT INFRATILE

BLUE LABEL
RECORDS·

350 CONEJO RIDGE AVENUE THOUSAND OAKS
CALIFORNIA **91361805** 370.5858 TEL
■ ZIP CODE 370.1202 FAX

WWW.BLUELABELRECORDS
URL.NET

BLUE LABEL
RECORDS

DAVE MASON
CO-FOUNDER

350 C
CALIFO
■ ZIP

BLUE LABEL
RECORDS

WWW.BLUELABELRECORDS.NET

BLUE LABEL
RECORDS

350 CONEJO RIDGE AVENUE THOUSAND OAKS
CALIFORNIA **91361805** 370.5858 TEL
■ ZIP CODE 370.1202 FAX

RKS DESIGN | ART DIRECTOR **RAVI K. SAWHNEY** | DESIGNER **ALEX MARQUES** | CLIENT **BLUE LABEL RECORDS**

2 San Francisco locations 3012 Fillmore Street 256 Sutter Street 415 788 3404 www.salonzendo.com

2 san francisco locations

3012 fillmore street 256 sutter street

415 788 3404 www.salonzendo.com

zendō

aveda salon spa boutique

2 san francisco locations

3012 fillmore street 256 sutter street

415 788 3404 www.salonzendo.com

Keven Thibeault

Operations Director

aveda salon spa boutique

zendō

zendō

aveda salon spa boutique

colleen o'mara
5225 wilshire blvd
suite 403
los angeles, ca 90036

tel 323 938 8363
fax 323 938 8757
colleen@hypeworld.com

5225 wilshire blvd

suite 403 los angeles

california 90036

tel 323 938 8363

fax 323 938 8757

SPECIAL MODERN DESIGN | ART DIRECTOR **KAREN BARRANCO** | CLIENT **HYPE**

PLUS DESIGN INC. | ART DIRECTOR **ANITA MEYER** | DESIGNERS **ANITA MEYER, VIVIAN LAW** | CLIENT **FINELINES**

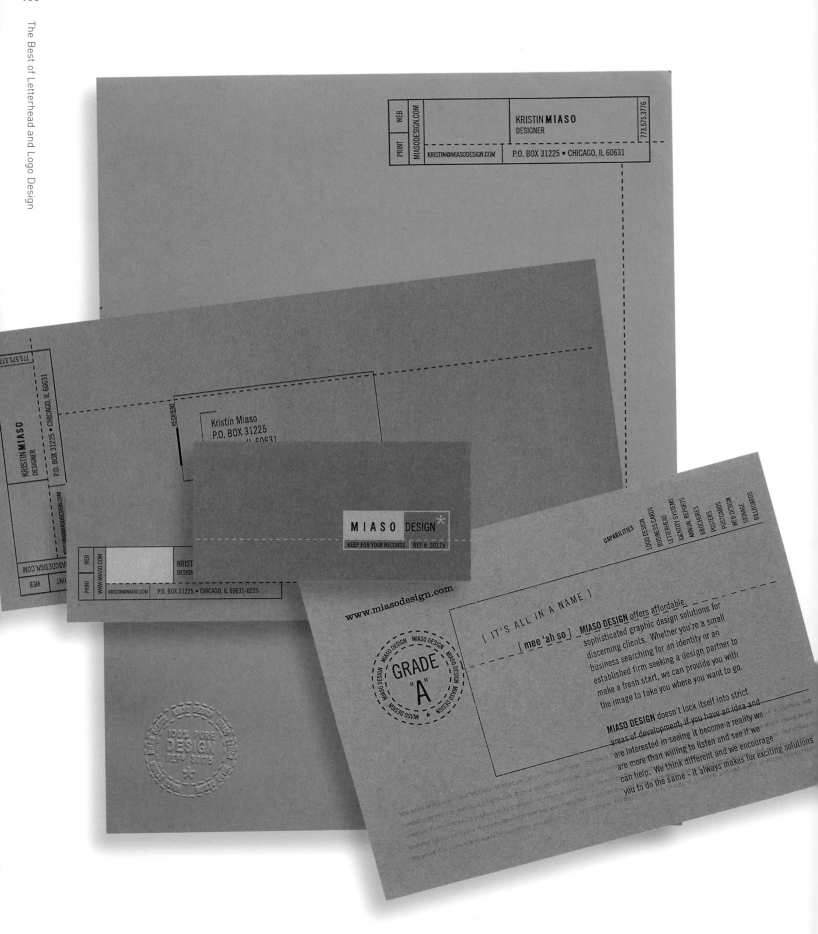

Backed by experts,
fronted by enthusias!

24/7

T 020 7556 1090
www.controlcircle.com

24hr support: 0870 990 9989

Blackwell House, Guildhall Yard, London EC2V 5AE.

control
circle

Car Park Limited trading as ControlCircle. Registered office: Blackwell House, Guildhall Yard, London EC2V 5AE.
Registered in England no 3976019. VAT reg 773 5777 80.

RE: SAL7MAN DESIGNS | ART DIRECTOR IDA CHEINMAN | DESIGNERS IDA CHEINMAN, RICK SALZMAN | CLIENT APEX SEO

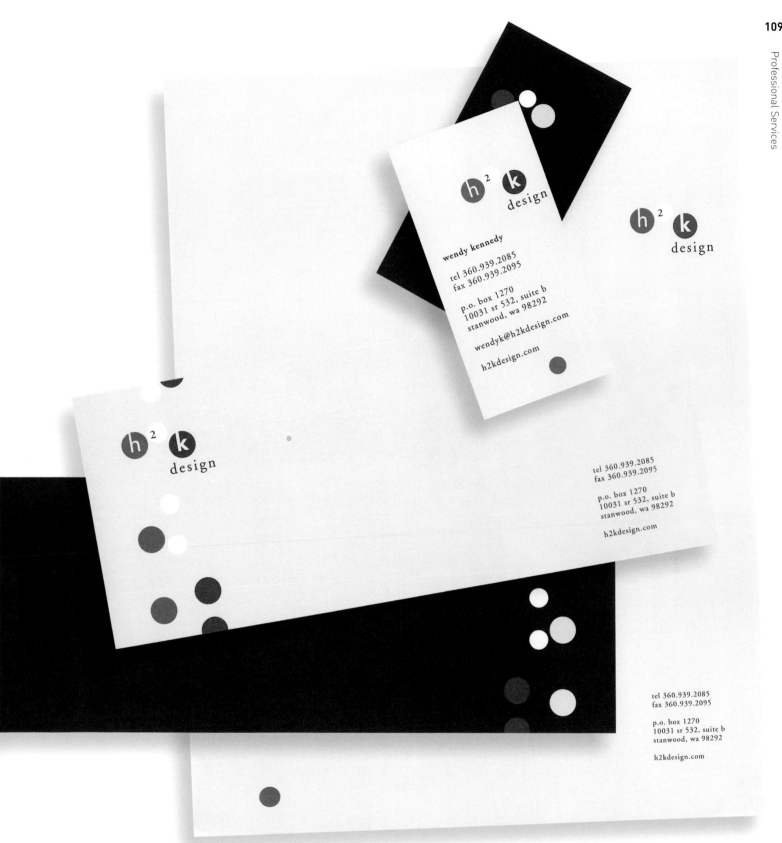

MONSTER DESIGN | DESIGNER HANNAH WYGAL | CLIENT **H2K** DESIGN

Die Konkurrenz

Die Konkurrenz

Andreas Palm

Die Konkurrenz
Agentur für
Kommunikation
GmbH

Geibelstraße 54
22303 Hamburg
Telefon 040.227 271-58
Fax 040.227 271-10
palm@werwardas.de

Die Konkurrenz

Die Konkurrenzveranstaltung

staltung

Die Konkurrenz
Agentur für
Kommunikation
GmbH

Geibelstraße 54
22303 Hamburg
Telefon 040.227 271-20´
Fax 040.227 271-10

Die Konkurrenz
im Internet
www.werwardas.de
info@werwardas.de

Die Konkurrenz
Agentur für
Kommunikation
GmbH

Geibelstraße 54
22303 Hamburg
Telefon 040.227 271-20
Fax 040.227 271-10

Die Konkurrenz im Internet
www.werwardas.de
info@werwardas.de

Hamburger Sparkasse
BLZ 200 505 50
Konto 1242.124 335

Geschäftsführer
Raphael Krickow
Handelsregister Hamburg
HRB 76471

LE-PALMIER | ART DIRECTOR ANDREAS PALM | CLIENT DIE KONHURRENZ AD AGENCY

THE DIECKS GROUP | ART DIRECTORS **MICHAEL WALDRON, BRIAN DIECKS** | DESIGNER **MICHAEL WALDRON** | CLIENT **SCANALOG**

making IT personal

qual

making IT personal

▶ networking
▶ security
▶ con...

qual
making IT personal

Patrick Stripp
Government Account Manager

Unit 10
Gatwick Metro Centre
Balcombe Road
Horley
Surrey
RH6 9GA

t: 01293 400 720
f: 01293 403 061

e: patrick@qual.co.uk
w: www.qual.co.uk

THOMAS BILLINGSLEY PHOTOGRAPHY

THOMAS BILLINGSLEY PHOTOGRAPHY

KARIZMA CULTURE | ART DIRECTOR **PERRY CHUA** | CLIENT **THOMAS BILLINGSLEY PHOTOGRAPHY**

LOCATED IN THE ANNEX / 45 ECCLES STREET OTTAWA ONTARIO K1R 6S3
613.567.7888 PHONE / 613.567.7528 FAX / csarchitect.com

Christopher Simmonds ARCHITECT

Christopher Simmonds ARCHITECT

WHITE SNOW ON VERMILLION BERRIES.
BUSY WINGS LOOSEN CRYSTAL SHOWER.

SILENCE.

LIGHT   AIR   WATER   EARTH

Christopher Simmonds ARCHITECT

THE ANNEX / 45 ECCLES STREET OTTAWA ONTARIO K1R 6S3
613.567.7888 X.22 PHONE / 613.567.7528 FAX / csarchitect.com
1.888.578.5678 TOLL FREE / pfiett@csarchitect.com

Pawel Fiett B.Arch. OAA

IRIDIUM, A DESIGN AGENCY | ART DIRECTORS JEAN-LUC DENAT, MARIO L'ECUYER | DESIGNER MARIO L'ECUYER | CLIENT CHRISTOPHER SIMMONDS

1

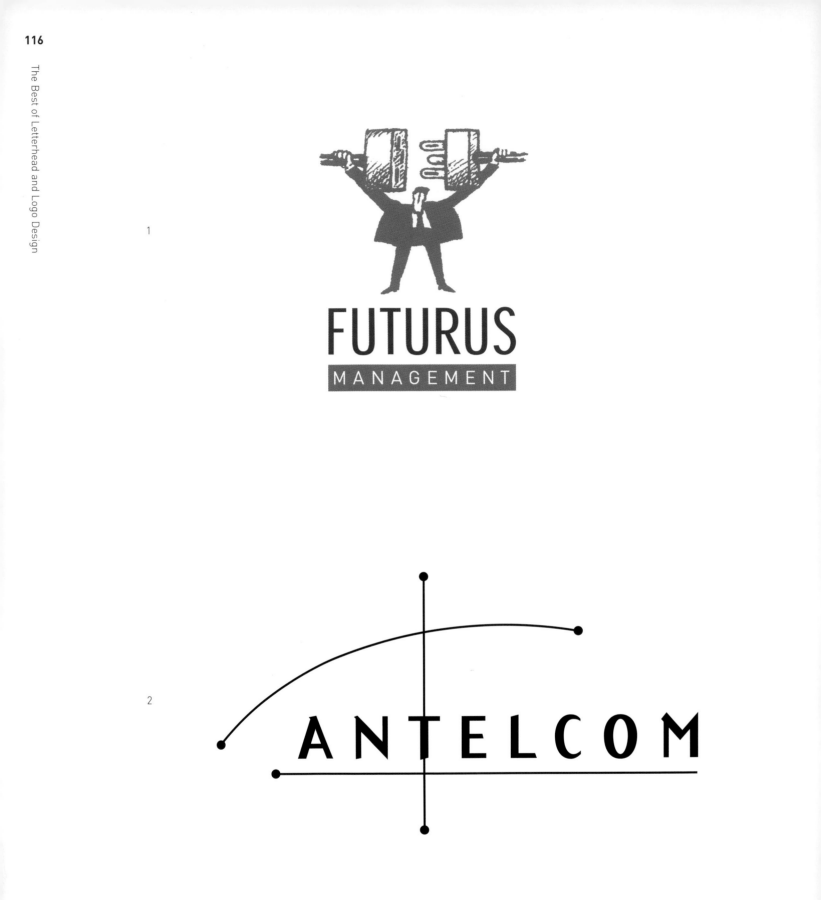

FUTURUS
MANAGEMENT

2

ANTELCOM

1 REACTOR ART + DESIGN | DESIGNERS PEBBLES CORREA, JERZY KOLACZ | CLIENT FUTURUS MANAGEMENT
2 MARC-ANTOINE HERRMANN | CLIENT ANTELCUM

Public Relations

Advertising

Interactive

Direct Marketing

fig 1a - www.anthillmarketing.com

Ant Hill
MARKETING

Ant Hill
MARKETING

P.O. Box 6585
Portland, Oregon 97228
ph (503) 236-3192
fx (503) 236-1186
kbrater@anthillmar

Ant Hill
MARKETING

P.O. Box 6585 · Portland, Oregon 97228 · ph (503) 236-3192 · fx (503) 236-1186

P.O. Box 6585 · Portland, Oregon 97228 · ph (503) 236-3192 · fx (503) 236-1186

PURE DESIGN INC. | ART DIRECTOR JOHN FISHER | CLIENT ANT HILL MARKETING

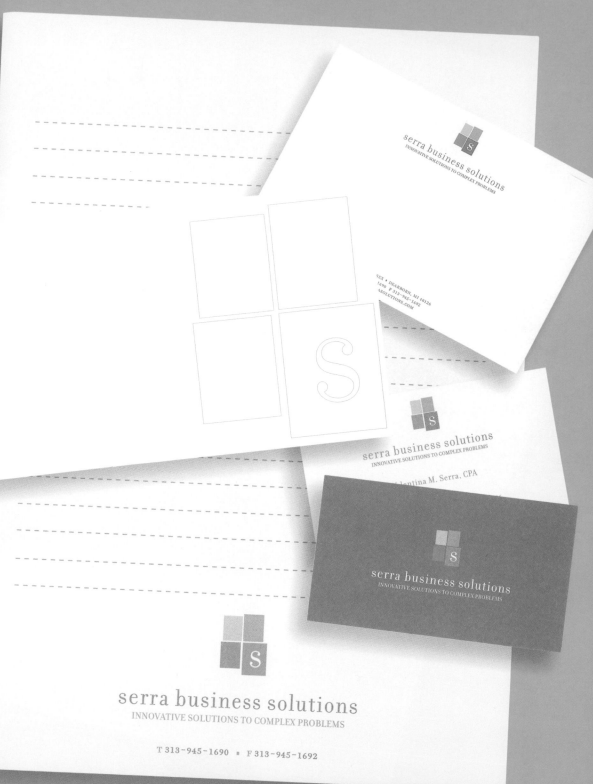

MIASO DESIGN | ART DIRECTOR KRISTIN MIASO | CLIENT SERRA BUSINESS SOLUTIONS

The Kenwood Group

The **Kenwood Group** 75 Varney Place, San Francisco, CA 94107 Tel 415 957-5333

The Kenwood Group

75 Varney Place
San Francisco, CA 94107
Tel 415 957-5333
Fax 415 957-5311

75 Varney Place, San Francisco, CA 94107 Tel 415 957-5333 Fax 415 957-5311 www.kenwoodgroup.com

THE DIECKS GROUP
530 BROADWAY, 9TH FLOOR
NEW YORK, NY 10012
STUDIO :: 212.226.7336
FAX :: 212.226.7937
www.diecksgroup.com

THE
DIECKS
GROUP
NEW YORK

brian@diecksgroup.com / www.diecksgroup.com

THE DIECKS GROUP
530 BROADWAY, 9TH FLOOR
NEW YORK, NY 10012

1 **GOTT FOLK McCANN-ERIKSUN** | ART DIRECTOR **EINAR GYLFASON** | CLIENT **SISSA PHOTOGRAPHY SCHOOL**
2 **LEWIS COMMUNICATIONS** | ART DIRECTOR **ROBERT FROEDGE** | CLIENT **STAGE POST VIDEO AND POST**

YOUR LIST   25 HAMPSTEAD LANE   TEL 0208 347 7816   WWW.YOURLISTLTD.COM
                LONDON N6 4RT   FAX 0208 342 8848   INFO@YOURLISTLTD.COM

REGISTERED NO. 4297981 REGISTERED OFFICE: 205/207 CRESCENT ROAD NEW BARNET HERTS EN4 8SB

NB STUDIO | ART DIRECTORS **NICK FINNEY, ALAN DYE, BEN STOTT** | DESIGNER **NICK VINCENT** | CLIENT **YOUR LIST**

Chapter 2:

CREATIVE SERVICES

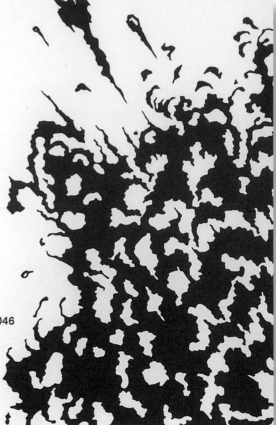

KIRIMA DESIGN Telephone 06-351-7045 Facsimile 06-351-7046

KIRIMA DESIGN Telephone 06-6351-7045 Facsimile 06-6351-7046

Yoriki-Cho Park-Bldg. 5F
1-5 Yoriki-Cho Kita-Ku Osaka-City
530-0036 Japan

キリマデザイン事務所
〒530-0036大阪市北区与力町1-5与力町パークビル5F

design firm	**Kirima Design Office**
art director	**Harumi Kirima**
designers	**Harumi Kirima, Fumitaka Yukawa**
client	**Kirima Design Office**

design firm	Seltzer Design
art director	Rochelle Seltzer
designers	Rochelle Seltzer, Heather Roy
client	Seltzer Design
tools	Quark XPress 3.32, Adobe Illustrator 7.01, Macintosh 8600 Power PC
paper/printing	Astrolite/Two color (IPMS, ITOYO)

128

design firm	**Hornall Anderson Design Works, Inc.**
art director	**Jack Anderson**
designer	**Mike Calkins**
client	**Hammerquist & Halverson**
tool	**Macromedia FreeHand**
paper/printing	**Mohawk, Navajo/Thermography on Business Card**

design firm | **Steven Curtis Design, Inc.**
art director | **Steve Curtis**
designer | **Steve Curtis**
client | **Steven Curtis Design, Inc.**
tools | **Quark XPress 4.0, Adobe Photoshop 5.0, Macintosh**
paper/printing | **Strathmore Writing, Ultra White Wove/ Anderson Printing**

design firm | **Plum Notion Design Laboratory**
art director | **Damion Silver**
designer | **Damion Silver**
client | **Plum Notion Design Laboratory**

5949 Sherry Lane   Suite 1800   Dallas, Texas 75225 | Phone 214.378.7970   Fax 214.378.7967

design firm	**The Point Group**
art director	**David Howard**
designers	**Crethann Hickman, Ridley Brown**
client	**The Point Group**
tools	**Quark XPress**
paper/printing	**Starwhite Vicksburg/Monarch Press**

design firm	**Gouthier Design, Inc.**
art director	**Jonathan Gouthier**
designer	**Jonathan Gouthier**
client	**Gouthier Design, Inc.**
tools	**Quark XPress, Macintosh Quadra**
paper/printing	**Neenah Classic Crest Solar White/Joanne Miner**

design firm	**Studio Hill**
art director	**Sandy Hill**
designers	**Sandy Hill, Alan Shimato**
client	**Studio Hill**
tools	**Quark XPress, Macintosh**
paper/printing	**70 lb. Mohawk Superfine Ultrawhite Eggshell Text**
	and 100 lb. Cover/Cottonwood Printing Co.

design firm | **Designstudio CAW**
designe | **Carsten-Andres Werner**
client | **Self-promotion**

DESIGNSTUDIO CAW   Carsten-Andres Werner | diplom grafikdesigner   kommunikationsgestaltung
Krugstraße 16 | 30453 Hannover | tel 0511.485.0295 | fax 0511.485.0299 | mail @designstudio-caw.de

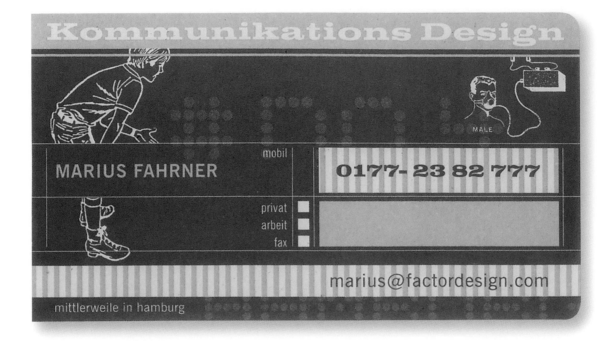

design firm	**Marius Fahrner**
art director	**Marius Fahrner**
designer	**Marins Fahrner**
client	**Self-promotion**
tool	**Macromedia FreeHand**
paper/printing	**Romerturm Countryside/Reset Hamburg**

design firm	Henderson Tyner Art Co.
art director	Troy Tyner
designer	Troy Tyner
client	Pam Fish
tool	Macromedia FreeHand
paper/printing	Strathmore Elements Grid/Topline Printing

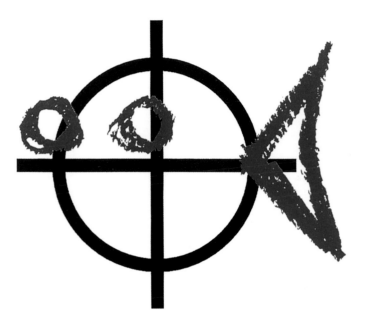

 m c g   a r c h i t e c t u r e

design firm	Selbert Perkins Design Collaborative
art director	Clifford Selbert
designers	Michelle Summers, Erin Miller
client	MCG Architects

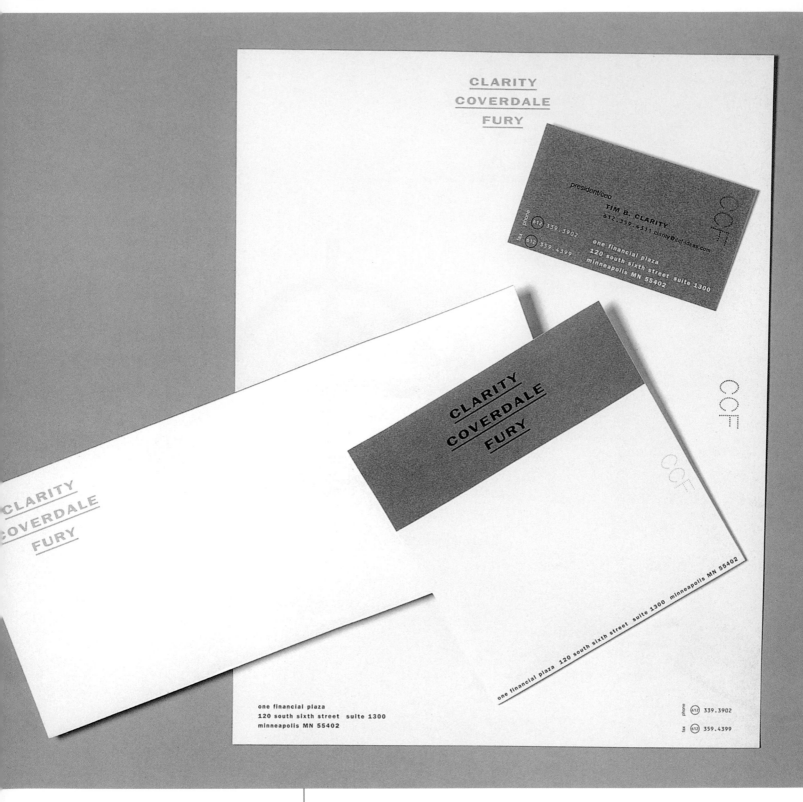

design firm | **Parachute Design**
designer | **Cari Johnson**
client | **Clarity Coverdale Fury Advertising**
tools | **Quark XPress, Macintosh Power PC**
paper/printing | **Mohawk Superfine/Offset with Lazer Cutting on Detail**

design firm	**Blue i Design**
art director	**Hellen Rayner**
designer	**Hellen Rayner**
client	**Blue i Design**
tools	**Quark XPress, Macromedia FreeHand, Macintosh**
paper/printing	**James River Classic Super Wove/ Cotswold Printing**

BLUE i DESIGN

Imperial House

Lypiatt Road

Cheltenham

Gloucestershire

GL50 2QJ

Telephone: 01242 234500

Fax: 01242 253360

ISDN: 01242 221587

email: info@bluei.co.uk

Blue i Design Limited

Registered Office:

Roberts House

2 Manor Road Ruislip

Middlesex

Registered in England

No. 3437151

<table>
design firm	**Sayegh Design**
art director	**Janelle Sayegh**
designer	**Janelle Sayegh**
client	**Sayegh Design**
tools	**Adobe Photoshop, Quark XPress, Macintosh**
paper/printing	**Neenah Classic Crest/Two color, Locke Printing Company**
</table>

design firm | **Pham Phu Design**
art director | **Oanh Pham Phu**
designer | **Renald Strobel**
client | **Riesle Technological Consultants**
paper/printing | **Two color**

lima design

215 HANOVER STREET
BOSTON, MASSACHUSETTS 02113
617-FOR-BEAN [367-2326]
617-367-1255 [FAX]
BEANS@LIMADESIGN.COM
WWW.LIMADESIGN.COM

design firm	**Lima Design**
designers	**Lisa McKenna, Mary Kiene**
client	**Lima Design**
tools	**Quark XPress, Macromedia FreeHand**
paper/printing	**Monadnock Caress/Shawmut Printing**

design firm	**McGaughy Design**
art director	**Malcolm McGaughy**
designer	**Malcolm McGaughy**
client	**McGaughy Design**
tools	**Macromedia FreeHand, Macintosh Power PC**
paper/printing	**Various/Rubber stamp**

BIGBEATGROUP

10 clairmont gardens   glasgow G3 7LW

TEL 0141 331 7600
FAX 0141 332 0336
E-MAIL big_beat@compuserve.com

printed on recycled paper   big beat group limited   registered in scotland no. 137725

design firm	**Scott Stern**
art director	**Jonathan Frewin**
designer	**Jonathan Frewin**
client	**Big Beat Group Holdings Ltd**
tool	**Adobe Photoshop**
paper/printing	**Four-color process, spot color, Spot UV varnish**

design firm	Visual Dialogue
art director	Fritz Klaetke
designers	Fritz Klaetke, Chris Reese
client	Visual Dialogue
tools	Quark XPress, Adobe Photoshop, Macintosh Power PC
paper/printing	Certificate Stock, Starwhite Vicksburg/Innerer
	Klang Press, Alpha Press

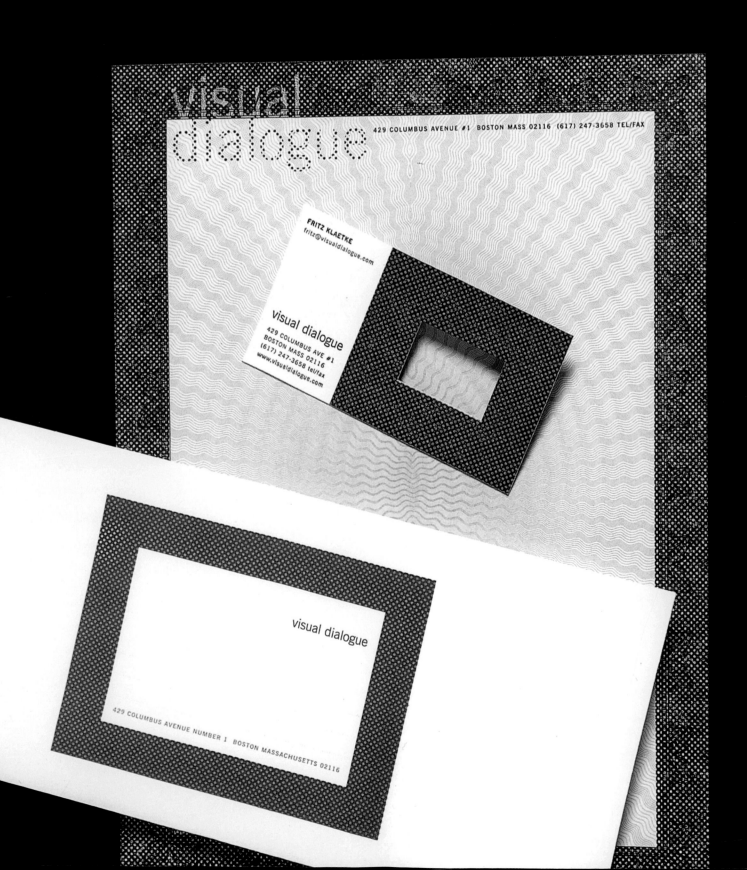

G3 Marketing und Kommunikation
Dr. Bernd Gschwandtner
Dr. Adolf-Altmann-Str. 17
A-5020 Salzburg

T +43-662-832601-0
F +43-662-832601-13
E g3-marketing@salzburg.co.at

design firm	**Modelhart Grafik-Design DA**
art director	**Herbert O. Modelhart**
designer	**Herbert O. Modelhart**
client	**G3 Marketing und Kommunikation**
tools	**Quark XPress, Adobe Illustrator**
paper/printing	**118 lb. Strathmore Writing/Two color**

---

design firm	**Lux Design**
art director	**Amy Gregg**
designer	**Laura Cary**
client	**Good Dog Design**
tools	**Adobe Illustrator, Macintosh 9600/300 Power PC**
paper/printing	**Starwhite Vicksburg/R.W. Nielsen Associates**

Good Dog Design

USA 114 Ryan Avenue Mill V...

AUSTRALIA 65 Princes Road Kingswood, SA 5062

Good Dog Design

65 Princes Road Kingswood, SA 5062 T 08.8373.5615 F 08.8373.3729 www.gooddogdesign.com

Good Dog Design

Henry Gooden
henry@gooddogdesign.com

65 Princes Road
Kingswood, SA 5062
Australia

T 08.8373.5615
F 08.8373.3729
www.gooddogdesign.com

good dog design

design firm	**Focus Design & Marketing Solutions**
art director	**Aram Youssefian**
designer	**Aram Youssefian**
client	**Focus**
tools	**Adobe Illustrator 7.0, Adobe Photoshop 4.0,**
	Macintosh G3
paper/printing	**Strathmore Writing System/Lithographix**

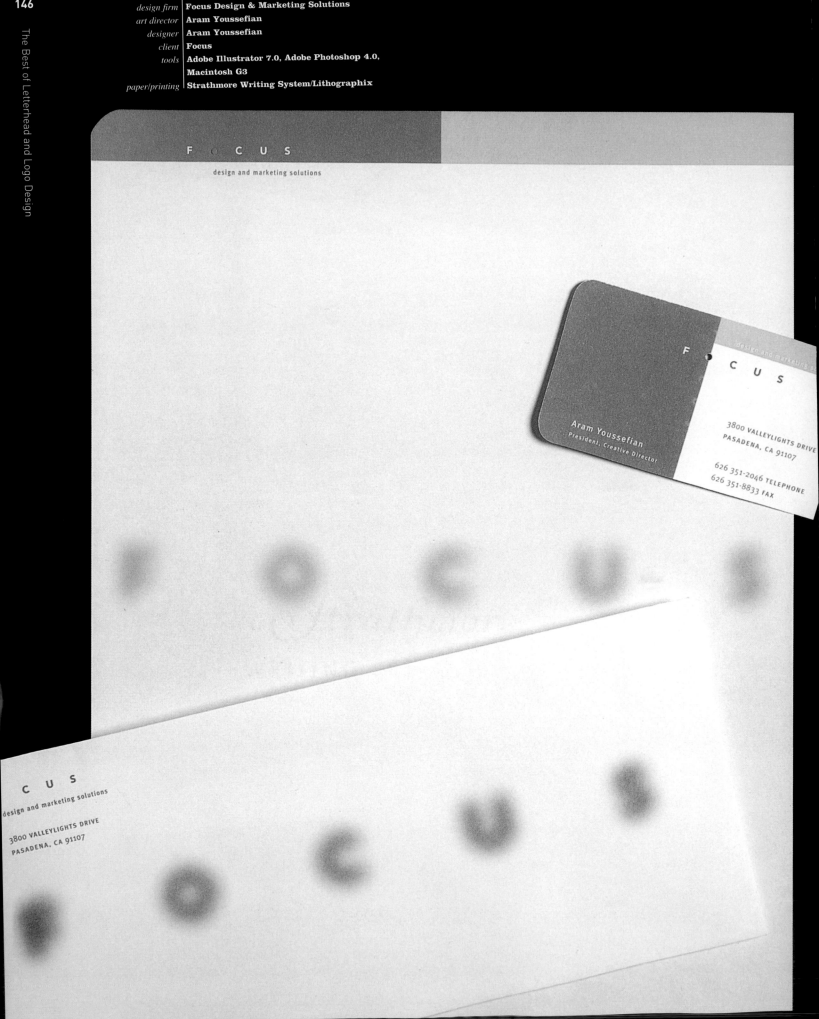

THE SOURCE OF THE FINEST
ARTISTS AND THEIR WORK

931 EAST MAIN STREET ▪ SUITE 3 ▪ MADISON ▪ WI ▪ 53703
PHONE 608.257.2590 ▪ FAX 608.257.2690 ▪ WWW.GUILD.COM

THE SOURCE OF THE FINEST
ARTISTS AND THEIR WORK

TONI SIKES
PRESIDENT

TSIKES@GUILD.COM
931 E. MAIN ST. ▪ STE. 3
MADISON ▪ WI ▪ 53703
PHONE ▪ 608.257.2590
FAX ▪ 608.257.2690

design firm	**Planet Design Company**
art director	**Dana Lytle**
designer	**Ben Hirby**
client	**Guild.com**
tools	**Adobe Illustrator, Quark XPress**
paper/printing	**Neenah Classic Crest Natural White/ American Printing**

design firm	**Planet Design Company**
art director	**Kevin Wade**
designer	**Dan Ibarra**
client	**Brave World Productions**
tools	**Adobe Photoshop, Adobe Illustrator,**
	Quark XPress
paper/printing	**Mohawk Vellum Warm White/**
	American Printing

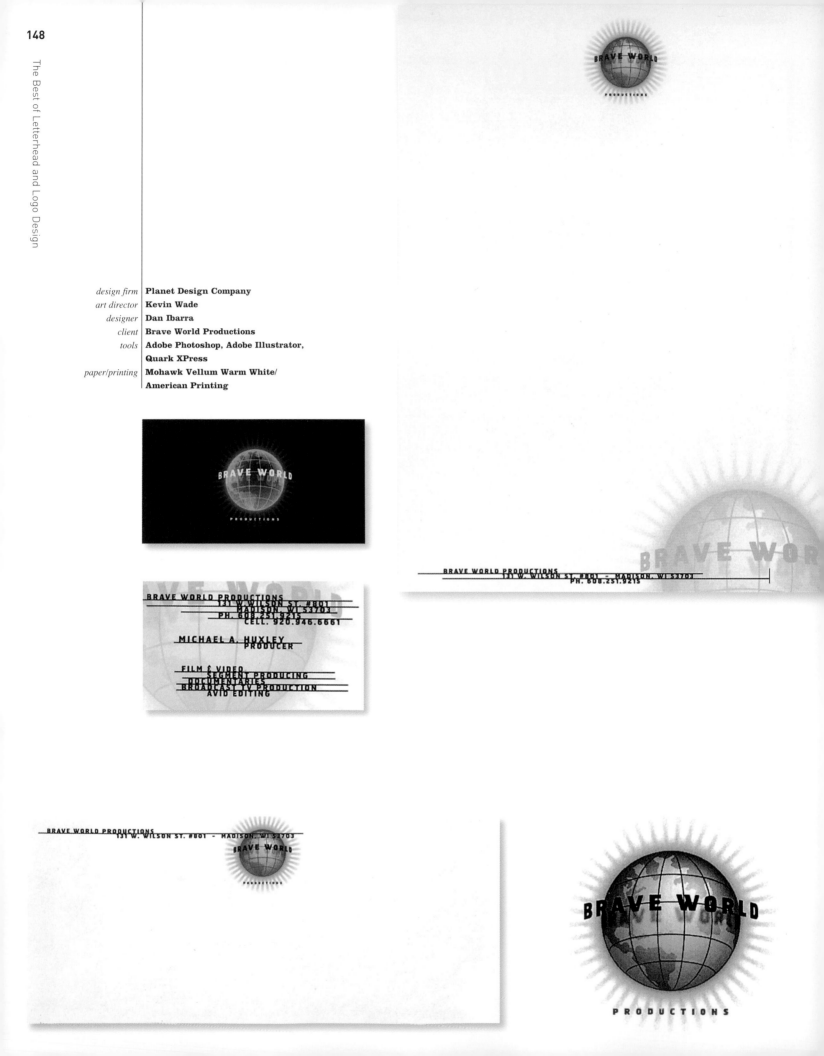

design firm | **Hornall Anderson Design Works, Inc.**
art director | **Jack Anderson**
designers | **Jack Anderson, David Bates**
client | **Hornall Anderson Design Works, Inc.**
tool | **Macromedia FreeHand**
paper/printing | **French Durotone, Packing Grey Liner;**
| **French Durotone, Newsprint White**

design firm	**Vestígio, Lda.**
art director	**Emanuel Barbosa**
designer	**Emanuel Barbosa**
client	**Vestígo**
tools	**Macromedia FreeHand, Macintosh 8100 Power PC**
paper/printing	**Favini/Two color**

design firm	**Roslyn Eskind Associates Limited**
art director	**Roslyn Eskind**
designer	**Roslyn Eskind**
client	**Roslyn Eskind Associates Limited**
tools	**Quark XPress, Adobe Photoshop, Adobe Illustrator, Macintosh**
paper/printing	**Chartham/Seaway Printing**

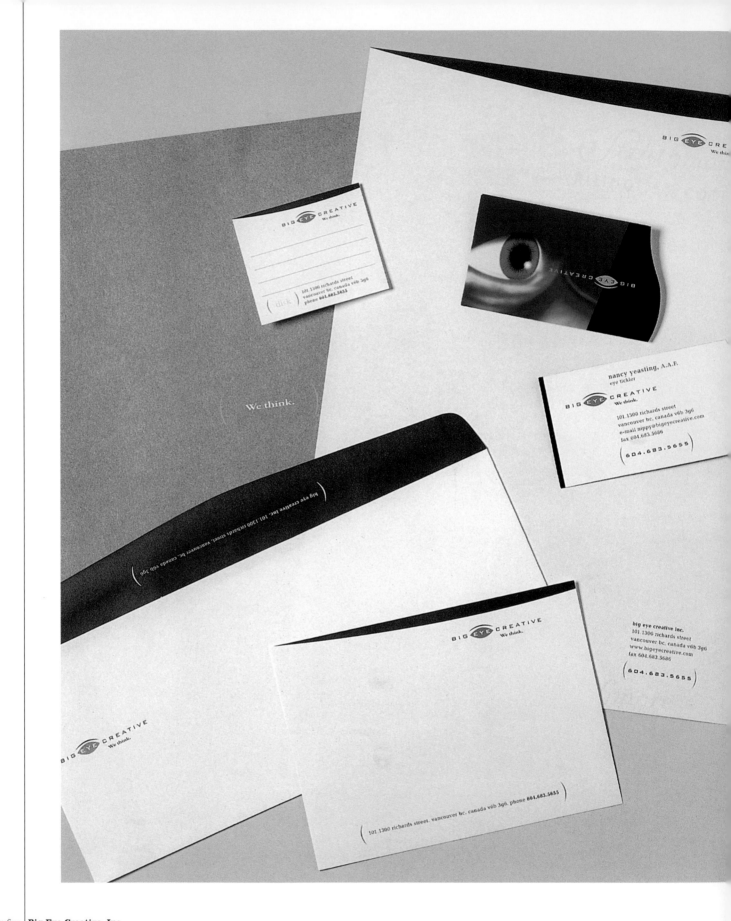

design firm	**Big Eye Creative, Inc.**
art director	**Perry Chua**
designer	**Perry Chua**
client	**Big Eye Creative, Inc.**
tools	**Adobe Illustrator 6.0, Adobe Photoshop 4.0,**
	Macintosh
paper/printing	**Cards: 120 lb. McCoy, Rest: Strathmore**
	Writing/Clarke Printing

RICHARDS ⬤ DESIGN GROUP INC

5616 Kingston Pike, Suite 105
Knoxville, Tennessee 37919-6325

Post Office Box 10773
Knoxville, Tennessee 37939-0773

423-588-9707 Telephone
423-584-7741 Facsimile

www.richardsdesign.com

design firm	**Richards Design Group, Inc.**
art director	**Michael Richards**
designer	**Timothy D. Jenkins**
client	**Richards Design Group**
tools	**Adobe Illustrator, Quark XPress**
paper/printing	**Strathmore Soft White Wove/Ullrich Printing**

Timothy D. Jenkins / Designer

RICHARDS ⬤ DESIGN GROUP INC

5616 Kingston Pike, Suite 105
Knoxville, Tennessee 37919-6325

Post Office Box 10773
Knoxville, Tennessee 37939-0773

423-588-9707 Telephone
423-584-7741 Facsimile

tjenkins@richardsdesign.com

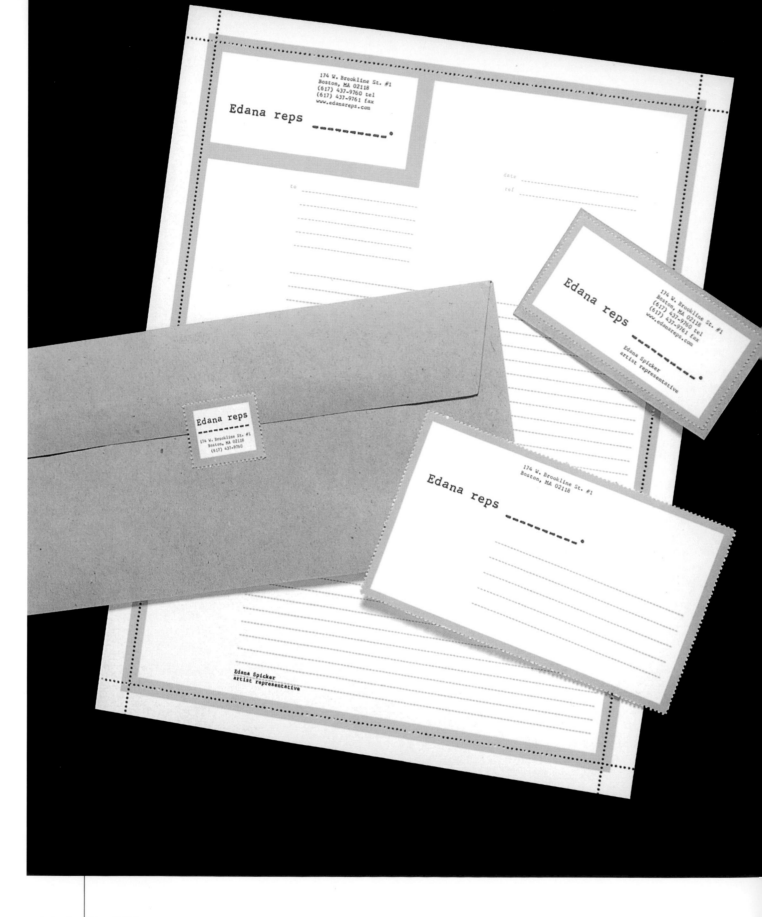

design firm | **Visual Dialogue**
art director | **Fritz Klaetke**
designer | **Fritz Klaetke**
client | **Edana Reps**
tools | **Quark XPress, Adobe Photoshop, Macintosh Power PC**
paper/printing | **Strathmore Writing & Labor Stock/Alpha Press**

design firm	Karacters Design Group
creative director	Maria Kennedy
designer	Matthew Clark
client	Karacters Design Group
tools	Adobe Illustrator, Quark XPress, Adobe Photoshop, Macintosh
paper/printing	Classic Crest/Hemlock Printing

exhibit a communications

Twenty-five
Corporate Dr
Suite 218
Burlington
MA 01803

Phone 781·
273·2999

Fax 781·
273·3733

www.exhibit-a.com
eac@exhibit-a.com

design firm	**Exhibit A Communications**
art director	**Mark Gedrich**
designer	**Mark Gedrich**
client	**Exhibit A Communications**
tools	**Adobe Illustrator, Macintosh 9500 Power PC**

ANNI KUAN

ANNI KUAN

242 W 38TH ST NEW YORK NY 10018 PHONE 212 704 4038 FAX 704 0651

ANNI KUAN

design firm	Sagmeister Inc.
art director	Stefan Sagmeister
designers	Stefan Sagmeister/Hjalti Karlsson
client	Anni Kuan Design
tools	Adobe Illustrator/Macintosh 9500 Power PC
paper/printing	Strathmore Writing/ Offset, Laser Die-Cut

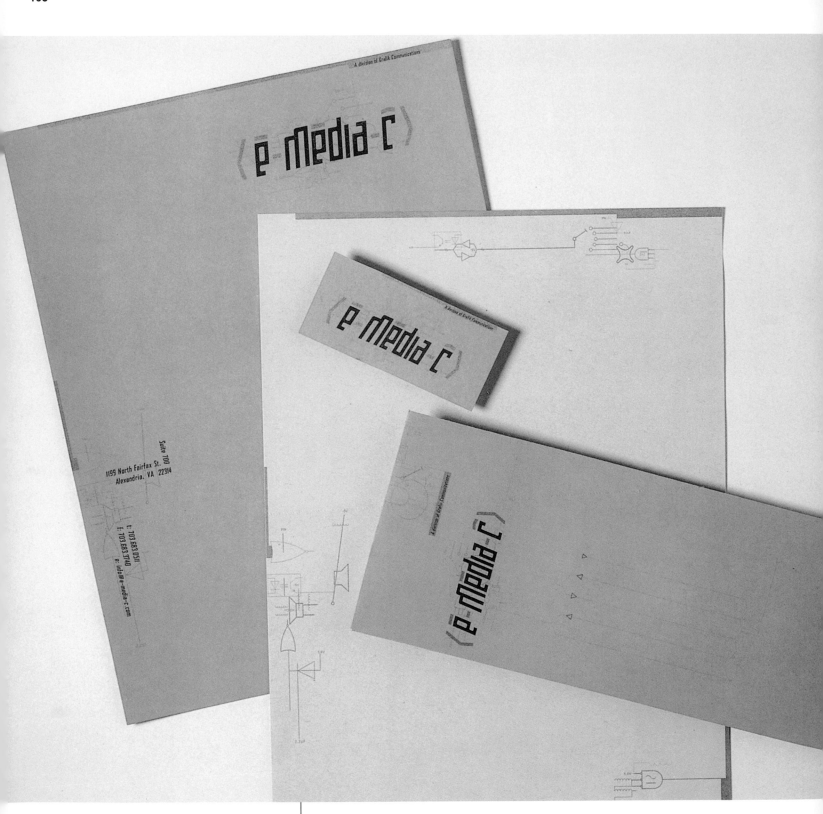

design firm | **Grafik Communications, Ltd.**
design team | **Jonathan Amen, Eric Goetz**
illustrator | **Jonathan Amen**
client | **E-Media-C**
tools | **Macromedia FreeHand, Quark XPress**
paper/printing | **French Construction Fuse Green & Cement Green**

DESIGN FIRM	A1 Design
DESIGNER	Amy Gregg
CLIENT	A1 Design
TOOLS	Adobe Illustrator, Macintosh

601 Minnesota studio 120
San Francisco, California 94107
Tel 415.824.9191 Fax 415.824.9454
amy@a1design.com

Amy Gregg

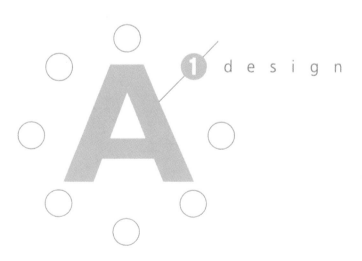

DESIGN FIRM	Anderson Thomas Design
ART DIRECTORS	Joel Anderson, Roy Roper
DESIGNER	Roy Roper
CLIENT	Anderson Thomas Design
TOOLS	Quark XPress, Adobe Illustrator, Adobe Photoshop

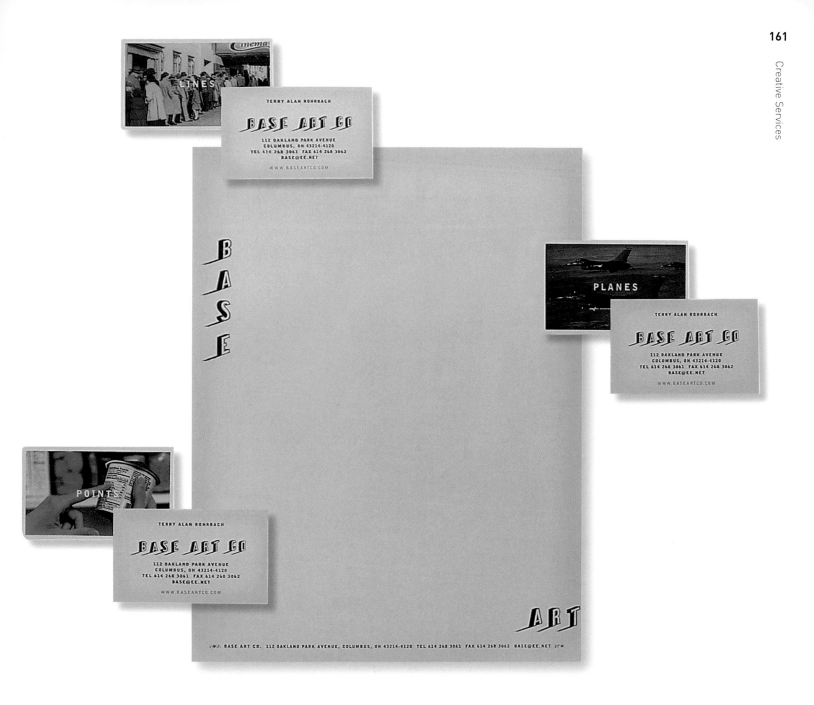

DESIGN FIRM	Base Art Co.
ART DIRECTOR	Terry Alan Rohrbach
DESIGNER	Terry Alan Rohrbach
CLIENT	Base Art Co.
TOOLS	Quark XPress, Macintosh

DESIGN FIRM	Buchanan Design
ART DIRECTOR	Bobby Buchanan
DESIGNERS	Armando Abundis, Bobby Buchanan
CLIENT	Buchanan Design
TOOLS	Adobe Illustrator, Macintosh

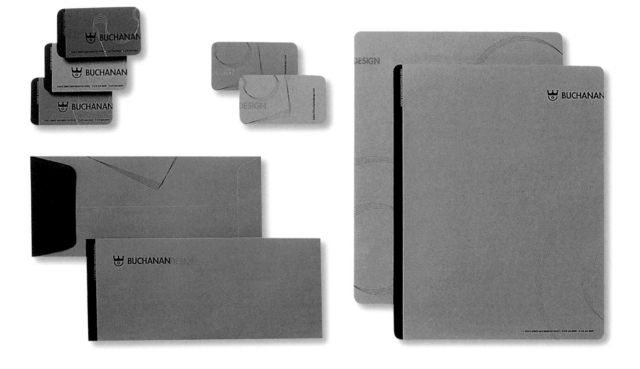

DESIGN FIRM	Bullet Communications, Inc.
ART DIRECTOR	Timothy Scott Kump
DESIGNER	Timothy Scott Kump
CLIENT	Bullet Communications, Inc.
TOOLS	Adobe Illustrator, Macintosh

TIMOTHY SCOTT KUMP
PRINCIPAL / CREATIVE DIRECTOR

BULLET COMMUNICATIONS, INC.®
200 S. MIDLAND AVE   JOLIET, ILLINOIS 60436
TEL: 815 741 2804   FAX: 815 741 2805
www.BulletCommunications.com
E-mail: 007@BulletCommunications.com

BULLET COMMUNICATION
200 S. MIDLAND AVE   JOLIET, ILL

www.BulletCommunications

BULLET COMMUNICATIONS, INC.®
200 S. MIDLAND AVE   JOLIET, ILLINOIS 60436   TEL: 815 741 2804   FAX: 815 741 2805
www.BulletCommunications.com   E-mail: 007@BulletCommunications.com

Bullet Communications, Inc., and its logo are registered service marks of Bullet Communications, Inc.

DESIGN FIRM | Becker Design
DESIGNER | Neil Becker
CLIENT | Charlton Photos, Inc.
TOOLS | Adobe Illustrator, Macintosh

DESIGN FIRM	Dynamo Design
DESIGNER	Alan Bennis
CLIENT	Design Partners
TOOLS	Adobe Illustrator, Adobe Photoshop, Quark XPress

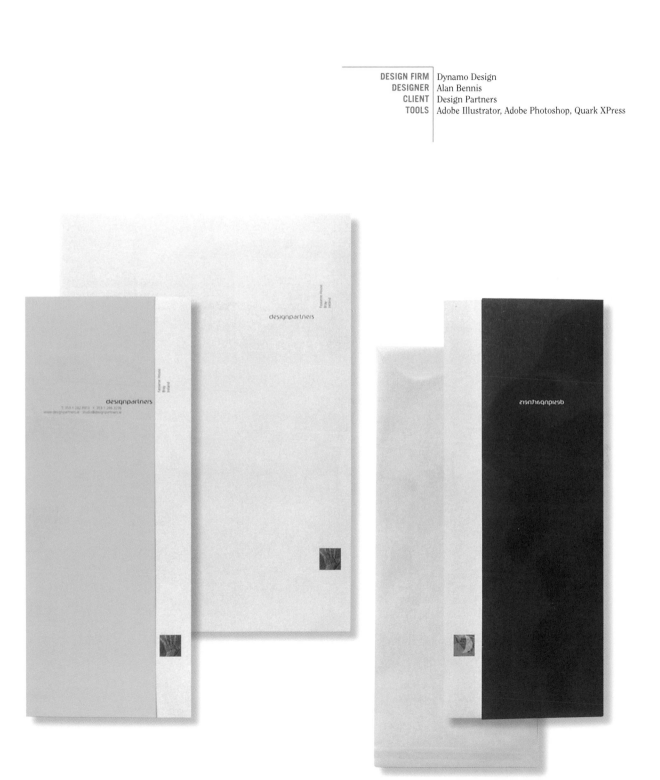

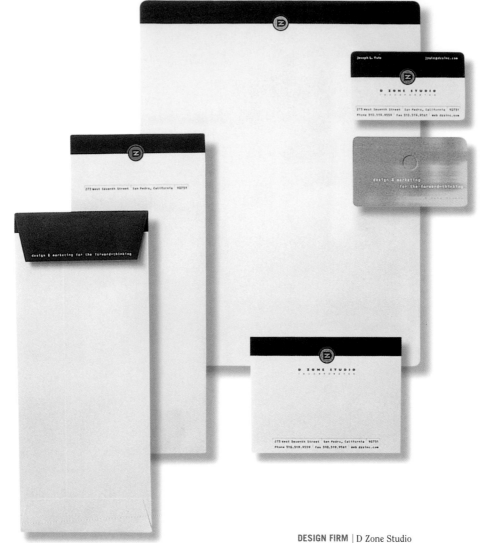

DESIGN FIRM	D Zone Studio
ART DIRECTOR	Joe Yule
DESIGNER	Joe Yule
CLIENT	D Zone Studio
TOOLS	Adobe Illustrator, Macintosh

DESIGN FIRM	Graphiculture
ART DIRECTOR	Cheryl Watson
DESIGNERS	Lindsay Little, Beth Mueller
CLIENT	Graphiculture
TOOLS	Quark XPress, Macromedia FreeHand

DESIGN FIRM	Gardner Design
ART DIRECTOR	Brian Miller
DESIGNER	Brian Miller
CLIENT	John Crowe Photography
TOOL	Macromedia FreeHand

JOHN

(CROWE)

DESIGN FIRM	Gardner Design
ART DIRECTORS	Bill Gardner, Brian Miller
DESIGNER	Brian Miller
CLIENT	Paul Chauncey Photography
TOOL	Macromedia FreeHand

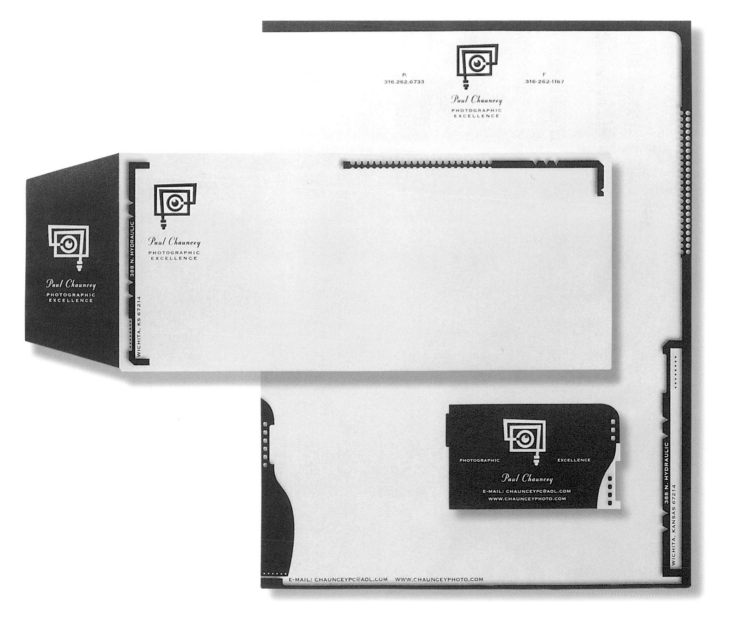

DESIGN FIRM | KAISERDICKEN
ART DIRECTOR | Craig Dicken
DESIGNERS | Craig Dicken, Debra Kaiser, Anthony Sini
CLIENT | Turtle Airways
TOOLS | Quark XPress, Adobe Illustrator, Adobe Photoshop, Macintosh

DESIGN FIRM	Jeff Fisher LogoMotives
ART DIRECTOR	Jeff Fisher
DESIGNERS	Jeff Fisher, Brett Bigham
CLIENT	Black Dog Furniture Design
TOOLS	Macromedia FreeHand, Macintosh

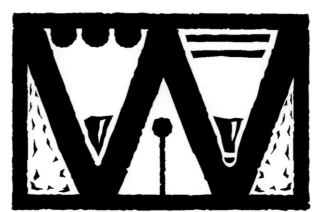

KIMBERLY WATERS

DESIGN FIRM	Jeff Fisher LogoMotives
ART DIRECTOR	Jeff Fisher
DESIGNER	Jeff Fisher
CLIENT	Kimberly Waters
TOOLSO	Macromedia FreeHand, Macintosh

DESIGN FIRM	Nassar Design
ART DIRECTOR	Nelida Nassar
DESIGNER	Margarita Encorienda
CLIENT	Nassar Design
TOOLS	Adobe Illustrator, Quark XPress, Adobe Photoshop

DESIGN FIRM	Oakley Design Studios
ART DIRECTOR	Tim Oakley
DESIGNER	Tim Oakley
CLIENT	Doug Baldwin, Copywriter
TOOL	Adobe Illustrator 7.0

DESIGN FIRM	Punkt
ART DIRECTOR	Giles Dunn
DESIGNER	Giles Dunn
CLIENT	Big Fish Design Consultants
TOOL	Macromedia FreeHand

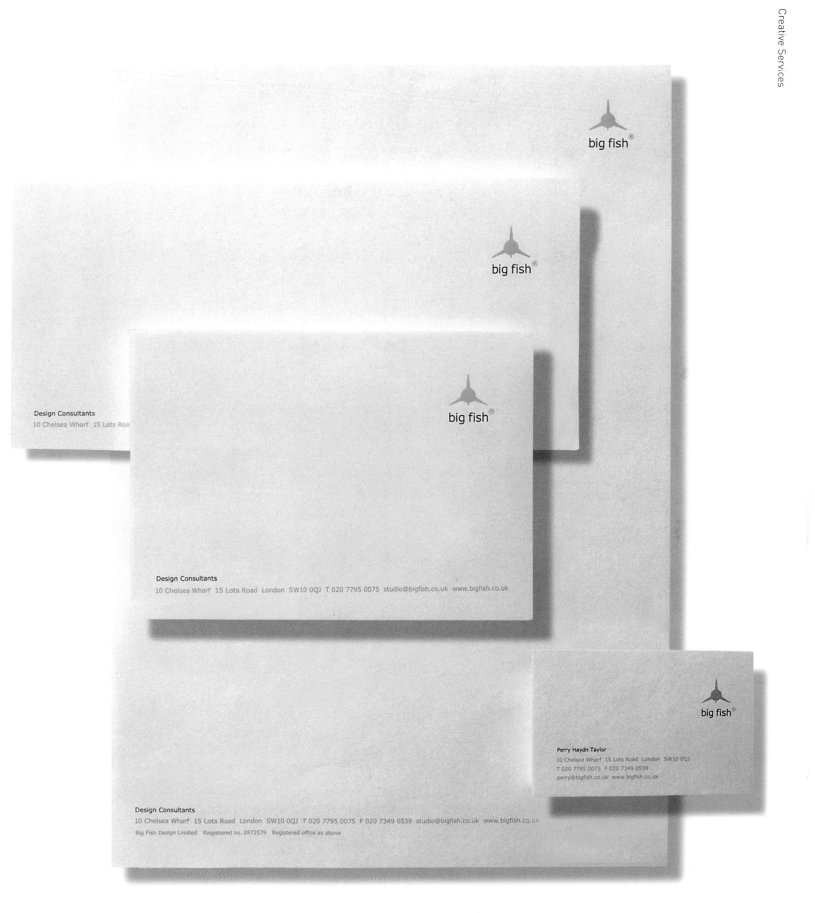

Design Consultants
10 Chelsea Wharf 15 Lots Roa

Design Consultants
10 Chelsea Wharf 15 Lots Road London SW10 0QJ T 020 7795 0075 studio@bigfish.co.uk www.bigfish.co.uk

Perry Haydn Taylor
10 Chelsea Wharf 15 Lots Road London SW10 0QJ
T 020 7795 0075 F 020 7349 0539
perry@bigfish.co.uk www.bigfish.co.uk

Design Consultants
10 Chelsea Wharf 15 Lots Road London SW10 0QJ T 020 7795 0075 F 020 7349 0539 studio@bigfish.co.uk www.bigfish.co.uk
Big Fish Design Limited   Registered no. 2972579   Registered office as above

DESIGN FIRM	PXL8R Visual Communications
PHOTOGRAPHER	Craig Molenhouse
DESIGNER	Craig Molenhouse
CLIENT	PXL8R Visual Communications
TOOLS	Adobe Photoshop, Adobe Illustrator, Quark XPress, Macintosh

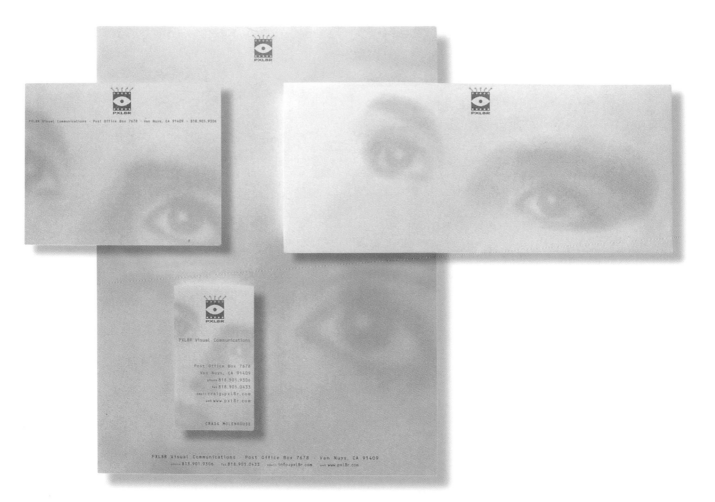

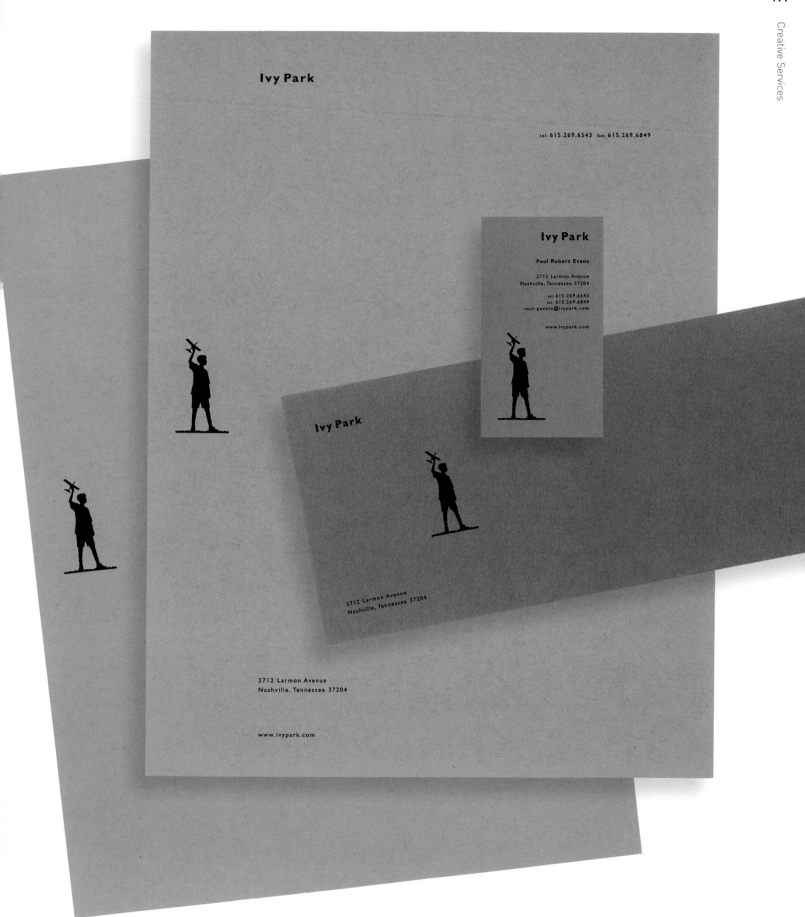

martinBattarchitects
Martin Batt
39 Wachusett Road
Needham
MA 02492
USA
Telephone 781 444 2747
Fax 781 444 0894
mbatt@martinbatt.com

martinBattarchitects
39 Wachusett Road
Needham
MA 02492
USA
Telephone 781 444 2747
Fax 781 444 0894
martin Batt architects LLC

martinBattarchitects
39 Wachusett Road
Needham
MA 02492
USA
Telephone 781 444 2747
Fax 781 444 0894
www.martinbatt.com

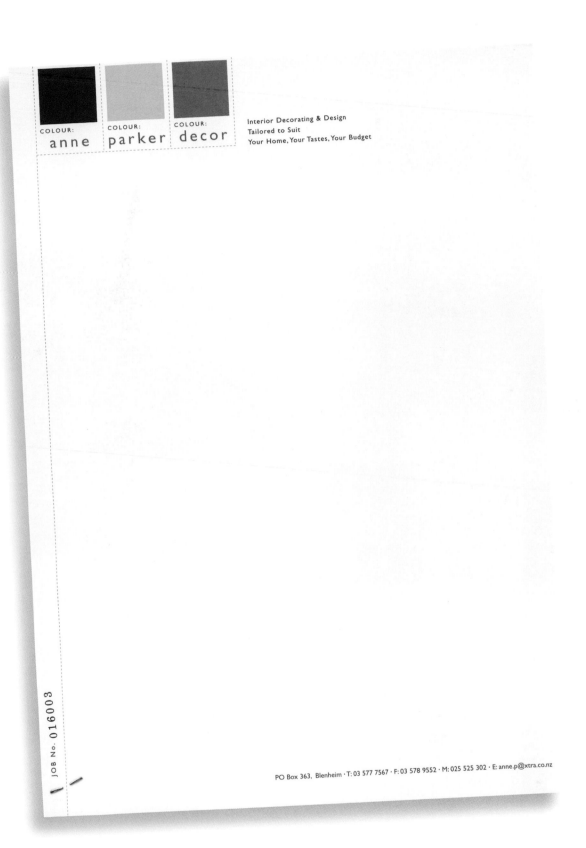

COLOUR:
COLOUR:
COLOUR:

anne | **parker** | **decor**

Interior Decorating & Design
Tailored to Suit
Your Home, Your Tastes, Your Budget

JOB No. 016003

PO Box 363, Blenheim · T: 03 577 7567 · F: 03 578 9552 · M: 025 525 302 · E: anne.p@xtra.co.nz

LLOYD'S GRAPHIC DESIGN AND COMMUNICATION | ART DIRECTOR **ALEXANDER LLOYD** | CLIENT **ANNE PARKER**

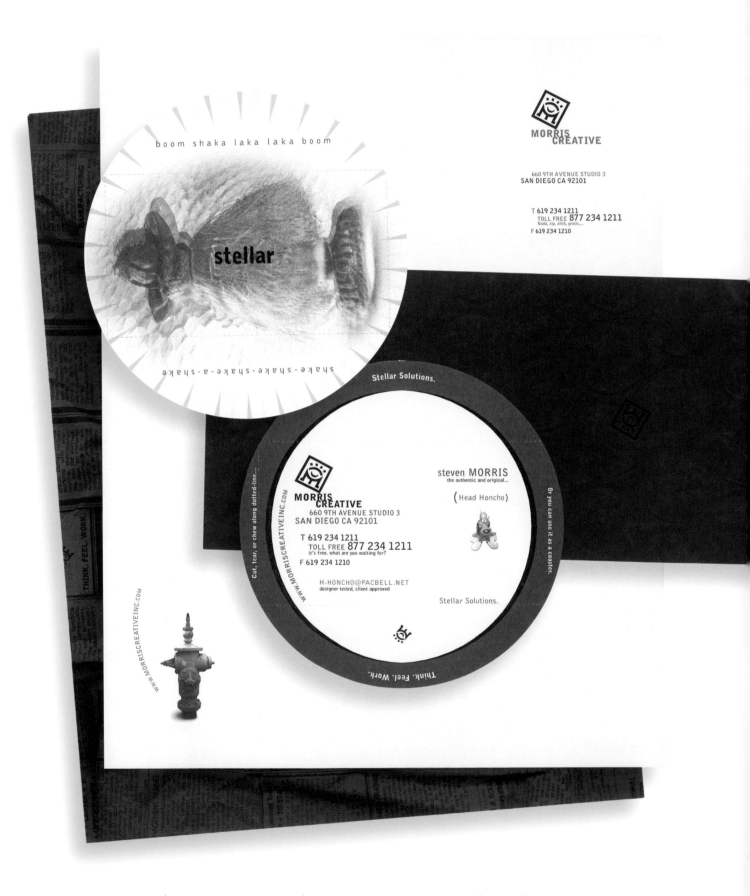

boom shaka laka laka boom

stellar

shake-shake-shake-a-shake

MORRIS
CREATIVE

660 9TH AVENUE STUDIO 3
SAN DIEGO CA 92101

T 619 234 1211
TOLL FREE 877 234 1211
Nada, zip, zilch, gratis,...
F 619 234 1210

Stellar Solutions.

MORRIS
CREATIVE
660 9TH AVENUE STUDIO 3
SAN DIEGO CA 92101

T 619 234 1211
TOLL FREE 877 234 1211
it's free. what are you waiting for?
F 619 234 1210

H-HONCHO@PACBELL.NET
designer tested, client approved

steven MORRIS
the authentic and original...

(Head Honcho)

Stellar Solutions.

Cut, tear, or chew along dotted-line...

WWW.MORRISCREATIVEINC.COM

Or you can use it as a coaster.

Think. Feel. Work.

THINK. FEEL. WORK.

WWW.MORRISCREATIVEINC.COM

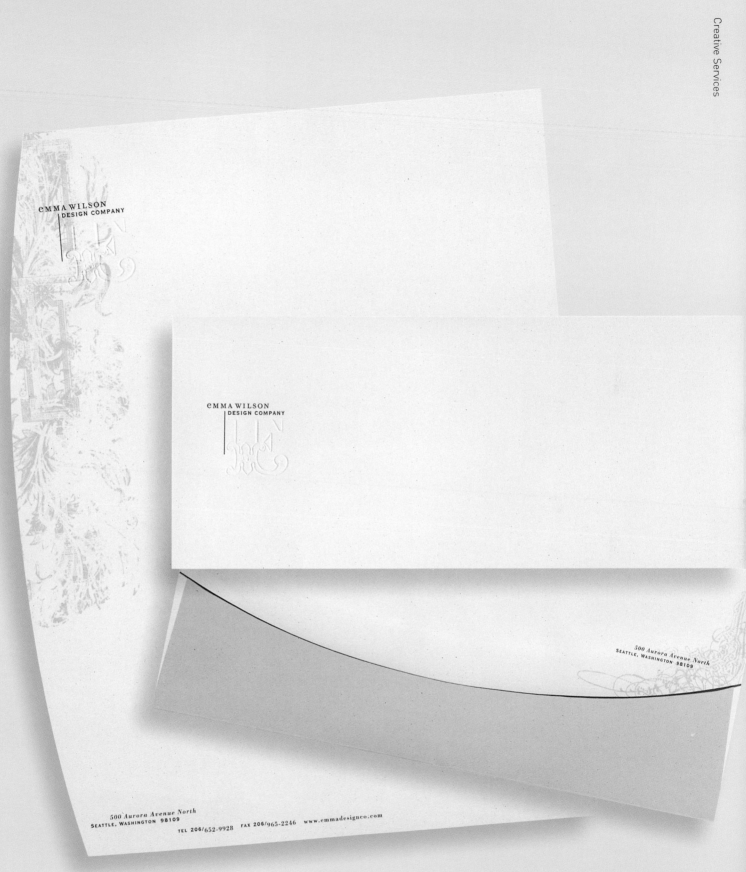

EMMA WILSON DESIGN CO. | DESIGNER EMMA WILSON | CLIENT EMMA WILSON DESIGN CO.

HeadQuarter.net

HEAD QUARTER | ART DIRECTORS **MARTIN BOTT, PETER HEINZ** | CLIENT HEAD QUARTER

HOLGER SCHEIBE // PHOTOGRAPHY

HOLGER SCHEIBE

HOLGER SCHEIBE

HAMBURG +49 40.430 41 75 // NEW YORK +1 212.213 95 39
HOLGERSCHEIBE@AOL.COM // WWW.HOLGERSCHEIBE.COM
GLASHÜTTENSTRASSE 38 // 20357 HAMBURG

HOLGER SCHEIBE // PHOTOGRAPHY

HAMBURG +49 40.430 41 75 // NEW YORK +1 212.213 95 39   GLASHÜTTENSTRASSE 38 // 20357 HAMBURG // FAX +49 40.432 26 14
HOLGERSCHEIBE@AOL.COM // WWW.HOLGERSCHEIBE.COM   DEUTSCHE BANK HAMBURG // KONTO 36 82 762 // BLZ 200 700 00

LE-PALMIER | ART DIRECTOR **ANDREAS PALM** | CLIENT **HOLGAR SCHEIBE PHOTOGRAPHY**

chase design group

chase design group

tel 323 668 1055   fax 323 668 2470

www.chasedesigngroup.com

2255 bancroft avenue los angeles california 90039

chase

chase design group

2255 bancroft ave los angeles ca 90039

tel 323 668 1055 fax 323 668 2470

www.chasedesigngroup.com

Margo Chase

creative director

margo@chasedesigngroup.com

chase

chase

CHASE DESIGN GROUP | ART DIRECTOR **MARGO CHASE** | CLIENT **CHASE DESIGN GROUP**

NO. 27 HOXTON STREET
LONDON N1 6NH
TELEPHONE + 44 (0) 20 7613 3886
FAX + 44 (0) 20 7729 8500
EMAIL name@pennyrich.co.uk
www.pennyrich.co.uk

VAT NO. 627 9237 14

PENNY**RICH**

PENNY**RICH**

NO. 27 HOXTON STREET
LONDON N1 6NH
TELEPHONE + 44 (0) 20 7613 3886
FAX + 44 (0) 20 7729 8500
EMAIL penny@pennyrich.co.uk
www.pennyrich.co.uk

D. DESIGN | ART DIRECTOR **DEREK SAMUEL** | CLIENT **PENNY RICH**

Prisma Imaging
Colour reprographics

Unit Thirty Three
Westfield Trading Estate
Midsomer Norton
Radstock BA3 4BS

Telephone 01761 418867
Facsimile 01761 419464
Email prisma@dircon.co.uk
Registered No. 3202188

NORTH BANK | ART DIRECTOR **SIMON CRYER** | CLIENT **PRISMA REPROGRAPHICS**

unstable

MADE IN THE BUNDESREPUBLIK

| TELEPHONE | TELEFAX | ISDN | ADDRESS |
| +49(40) 432 948 - 0 | +49(40) 432 948 - 11 | +49(40) 432 948 - 31 | Juliusstrasse 25 | 22769 Hamburg |

FORK UNSTABLE MEDIA - 4RK   (NY) (HH) (B)

E.MAIL: INFO@FORK.DE   HTTP://WWW.FORK.DE

MADE IN THE BUNDESREPUBLIK   NY HH B

FORK UNSTABLE MEDIA - 4RK

>> HAMBURG >> NEW YORK >> BERLIN

FORK UNSTABLE MEDIA   NY HH B

NY   FORK UNSTABLE MEDIA

MAIL	jeremy@fork.de	INTERNET	http://www.fork.de
ADDRESS	184 Kent Avenue	TELEPHONE	+1 (718) 384 1401
FORK NEW YORK	Fifth floor, #5B	TELEFAX	+1 (718) 384 1402
	Brooklyn, NY 11211		

MADE IN THE BUNDESREPUBLIK

YELIZ ATILGAN PROJECT MANAGER   01

>> HAMBURG >> NEW YORK >> BERLIN

>>MOBILE   CRYSTAL

NOW LOADING

BANK Deutsche Bank Hamburg | BLZ 200 700 24 KTO 322 10 66
Fork Unstable Media GmbH

MARIUS FAHRNER DESIGN | ART DIRECTOR MARIUS FAHRNER | CLIENT FORK UNSTABLE MEDIA

DAN LIM SUZY JOHNSTON REP

suzy@danlimphoto.com
TEL 416.863.5115
TOLL FREE 877.737.7464
FAX 416.863.0890

www.danlimphoto.com

danlim

90 Sumach Street #617
Door Code #630
Toronto, ON Canada
M5A 4R4

suzy@danlimphoto.com

416.863.5115 TEL
877.737.7464 TOLL FREE
416.863.0890 FAX

www.danlimphoto.com

www.danlimphoto.com

danlim
photography

danlim
photography

90 Sumach Street #617, Toronto, ON Canada M5A 4R4

www.GARYBASEMAN.COM
BASEMANART @ EARTHLINK.NET

257 SOUTH LUCERNE BLVD, LOS ANGELES, CA 90004

BASEMAN

BASEMA
PH (323) 934-5567

BASEMAN
PH (323) 934-556

BLVD, LOS ANGELES, CA 90004
934-5516
K.NET

BASEMAN
PH (323) 934-5567

GARY BASEMAN | ART DIRECTOR **GARY BASEMAN** | DESIGNER **JILL VON HARTMANN** | CLIENT **GARY BASEMAN**

kevduttonphotography

57 Dorchester Court
London
SE24 9QY

T/F 020 7274 3337
M 07973 113969
E kevdutton@aol.com

VAT reg 681 5010 56

WILSON HARVEY | ART DIRECTOR **PAUL BURGESS** | DESIGNER **DAN ELLIOTT** | CLIENT **KEV DUTTON PHOTOGRAPHY**

www.lepalmier.de

Le_Palmier

Andreas Palm Design

Palmier

Le_Palmier
Andreas Palm Design
Große Brunnenstraße 63a

22763 Hamburg

www.lepalmier.de

Fon_040.460 690-61 : Fax_040.460 690-62
Große Brunnenstraße 63a : 22763 Hamburg
eMail_design@lepalmier.de

Andreas Palm Design

Le_Palmier

Fon_040.460 690-61 : Fax_040.460 690-62
Große Brunnenstraße 63a : D_22763 Hamburg
eMail_design@lepalmier.de

Chapter 3:

RETAIL, RESTAURANT, AND HOSPITALITY

design firm | **Hornall Anderson Design Works, Inc.**
art director | **Hornall Anderson Design Works, Inc.**
designers | **Larry Anderson, Mary Hermes,**
| **Mike Calkins, Michael Brugman**
client | **U.S. Cigar**
tools | **Macromedia FreeHand**

design firm	**Barbara Chan Design**
art director	**Barbara Chan**
designer	**Barbara Chan**
client	**Recess**
tools	**tools Adobe Illustrator 7.0, Macintosh G3**

design firm	**Kirima Design Office**
art director	**Harumi Kirima**
designer	**Harumi Kirima**
client	**Happy-En**

design firm	Jim Lange Design
art director	Lee Langill
designer	Jim Lange
client	Lee Langill
tool	Macintosh

design firm	Murrie Lienhart Rysner
art director	Linda Voll
designer	Linda Voll
client	Wellness Business Works
tool	Adobe Illustrator

393 Totten Pond Road
Waltham, MA 02451
(781)487-9996 direct
(781)487-9997 fax
(877)363-9463 gift orders
SENDWINE.COM website

design firm | **Phillips Design Group**
art director | **Steve Phillips**
designers | **Alison Goudreault, Susan Logher**
client | **Sendwine.com**
tools | **Adobe Illustrator 7.0, Macintosh G3**
paper/printing | **Strathmore Writing, Soft White/**
BHF Printing

198

design firm | **Arrowstreet Graphic Design**
art director | **Bob Lowe**
designer | **Seth Londergan**
client | **Pet Corner, LLC**
tools | **Adobe Illustrator, Macintosh Power PC**
paper/printing | **Poseidon White/Direct Printing**

design firm	**Vestígio**
art director	**Emanuel Barbosa**
designer	**Emanuel Barbosa**
client	**Latido**
tool	**Macromedia FreeHand**
paper/printing	**Renova Print/Two-color offset**

Name	RALPH ALTHOFF		PHON	+49 (0) 821 - 59 29 58		
			PHAX	+49 (0) 821 - 59 29 58		Logo
Adress	Alpenstraße 18	Bank	BfG Bank AG Augsburg			
	86159 Augsburg		BLZ 720 10 111			
	Germany		Kto 1422 6775 00	NO:	763	

RENT A BAR
Cocktails

» » RENT A BARMAN · Ralph Althoff · Alpenstraße 18 · 86159 Augsburg

» RENT A BAR VERANSTALTUNGSSERVICE «

design firm	**Marius Fahrner**
art director	**Marius Fahrner**
designer	**Marius Fahrner**
client	**'Rent a Bar' Barservice**
tools	**Adobe Illustrator, Quark XPress**
paper/printing	**Romerturm Countryside/**
	Schickinger Werbedrull 2/0

design firm	Vrontikis Design Office
art director	Petrula Vrontikis
designers	Christina Hsaio, Stationary: Petrula Vrontikis
client	Kozo Hasegawa, Global Dining, Inc.
tools	Adobe Photoshop, Quark XPress
paper/printing	Crosspointe Synergy/Login Printing

1212 3rd Street Promenade

Santa Monica, CA 90401

fax: (310) 576-9988
www.global-dining.com

phone: (310) 576-9996

design firm	**Mires Design**
art director	**John Ball**
designers	**John Ball, Miguel Perez, and Jeff Samaripa**
client	**dab fragrance sampling**

D I V A N

7661 GIRARD AVE. LA JOLLA, CALIFORNIA 92037 PH 619.551.0405 FAX 619.551.0639

design firm	Miriello Grafico, Inc.
art director	Ron Miriello
designer	Courtney Mayer
client	Divan
tools	Adobe Illustrator, Adobe Photoshop, Macintosh
printing	Offset litho three color over two color

boston Light source

Architectural Light
Manufacturer's Rep

64 commercial wharf, Boston, Massachusetts 02110-3808

7.367.0910

FAX: 617.367.0925

WEB: www.bostonligh

boston Light source

ROBERT A. EDWARDS

64 commercial wharf, Boston, MA 02110-3808

WEB: www.bostonlightsource.com

Architectural Lighting
Manufacturer's Representative

PHONE: 617.367.0910 x234 FAX: 617.367.0925

EMAIL: redwards.bls@lighting.net

on Light source

64 commercial wharf, Boston, MA 02110-3808

boston Light source

64 commercial wharf, Boston, MA 02110-3808

Representing manufacturers offering products with a perceptible
advantage for the coordination of lighting with architecture.

design firm | Korn Design
art director | Denise Korn
designer | Christine Brooks
client | Boston Light Source
tools | Adobe Illustrator, Quark XPress
paper/printing | Alpha Pressa

DESIGN FIRM | art+corporate culture
DESIGNER | Mag. Lothar Amilian Heinzle
CLIENT | Markus Maier
TOOLS | Macromedia FreeHand, Quark XPress

DESIGN FIRM	ARTiculation Group & Benchmark Porter Novelli
ART DIRECTOR	Joseph Chan
DESIGNER	Joseph Chan
CLIENT	The Shopping Channel
TOOL	Adobe Illustrator

DESIGN FIRM	Becker Design
DESIGNER	Neil Becker
CLIENT	A Food Affair
TOOLS	Adobe Illustrator, Macintosh

DESIGN FIRM	Bailey/Franklin
ART DIRECTOR	Dan Franklin
DESIGNER	Alex Epp
CLIENT	Boyd Coffee Company
TOOL	Macromedia FreeHand

DESIGN FIRM	Bruce Yelaska Design
ART DIRECTOR	Bruce Yelaska
DESIGNER	Bruce Yelaska
CLIENT	Hunan Garden
TOOLS	Adobe Illustrator, Macintosh

DESIGN FIRM | cincodemayo
ART DIRECTOR | Mauricìo Alanis
DESIGNER | Mauricìo Alanis
CLIENT | Phone City
TOOLS | Macromedia FreeHand, Macintosh

DESIGN FIRM	Cato Partners
DESIGNER	Cato Partners
CLIENT	Poppy Industries Pty. Ltd.
TOOLS	Adobe Illustrator 6, Macintosh

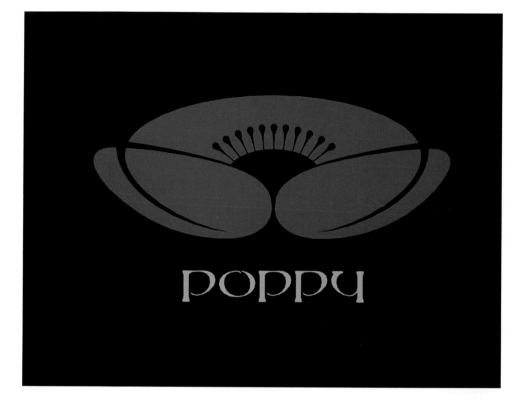

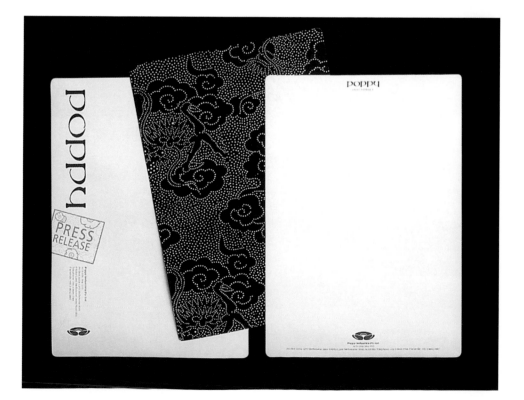

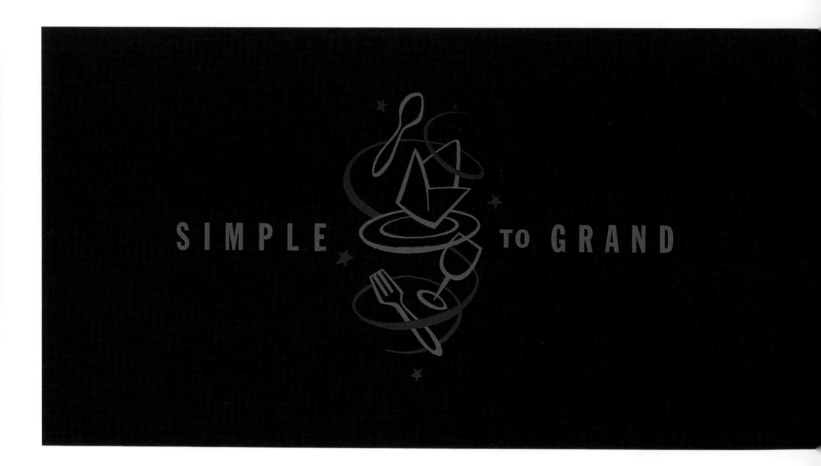

DESIGN FIRM	Design Center
ART DIRECTOR	John Reger
DESIGNER	Sherwin Schwartzrock
CLIENT	Simple to Grand
TOOLS	Macromedia FreeHand, Macintosh

DESIGN FIRM	Design Center
ART DIRECTOR	John Reger
DESIGNER	Cory Docken
CLIENT	Photoman
TOOLS	Macromedia FreeHand, Macintosh

DESIGN FIRM	DogStar
ART DIRECTOR	Lynn Smith/Perry, Harper & Perry Advertising
DESIGNER	Rodney Davidson
CLIENT	San Roc Cay Resort
TOOL	Macromedia FreeHand 7

DESIGN FIRM	Gardner Design
ART DIRECTOR	Bill Gardner
DESIGNER	Bill Gardner
CLIENT	Plazago
TOOL	Macromedia FreeHand

DESIGN FIRM	Gardner Design
ART DIRECTOR	Chris Parks
DESIGNER	Chris Parks
CLIENT	Big Fish
TOOL	Macromedia FreeHand

DESIGN FIRM	Gardner Design
ART DIRECTORS	Travis Brown, Bill Gardner
DESIGNER	Travis Brown
CLIENT	Iron Easel
TOOL	Macromedia FreeHand

Slow Cooked • Easy to Prepare
BUTCHER & COOK'S
Marinated • Great Tasting
Post Office Box 2519
Wichita, Kansas 67201
PO Box 2519 Wichita, KS 67201 • e-mail: butchercooks@
the everyday

DESIGN FIRM	Hornall Anderson Design Works, Inc.
ART DIRECTORS	Larry Anderson, Jack Anderson
DESIGNERS	Jack Anderson, Larry Anderson, Bruce Stigler,
	Bruce Branson-Meyer, Mary Chin Hutchison,
	Michael Brugman, Ed Lee, Kaye Farmer
CLIENT	Widmer Brothers
TOOL	Macromedia FreeHand

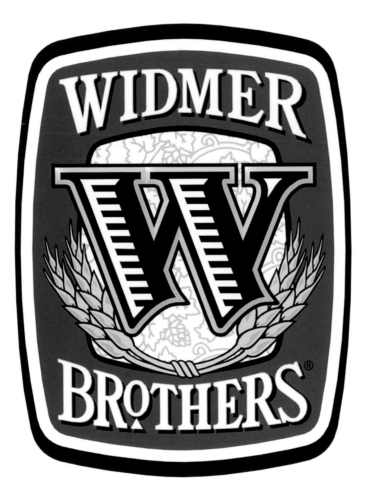

DESIGN FIRM	Gardner Design
ART DIRECTORS	Brian Miller, Bill Gardner
DESIGNER	Brian Miller
CLIENT	Butcher & Cooks
TOOLS	Macromedia FreeHand, Adobe Photoshop

COUGAR MOUNTAIN

GOURMET COOKIES

DESIGN FIRM	Hornall Anderson Design Works, Inc.
ART DIRECTORS	Jack Anderson, Debra McCloskey
DESIGNERS	Jack Anderson, Debra McCloskey, Lisa Cerveny, Mary Chin Hutchison, Gretchen Cook, Holly Craven, Dorothee Soechting
CLIENT	Cougar Mountain Cookies
TOOL	Macromedia FreeHand

DESIGN FIRM	Hornall Anderson Design Works, Inc.
ART DIRECTOR	Jack Anderson
DESIGNERS	Jack Anderson, Kathy Saito, Mary Chin Hutchison, Alan Copeland
CLIENT	Big Island Candies
TOOL	Macromedia FreeHand

DESIGN FIRM	Hornall Anderson Design Works, Inc.
ART DIRECTOR	Lisa Cerveny
DESIGNERS	Lisa Cerveny, Michael Brugman, Rick Miller, Belinda Bowling, Mary Hermes
CLIENT	Hardware.com
TOOL	Adobe Illustrator

DESIGN FIRM	Halleck
ART DIRECTORS	Daniel Tang, Wayne Wright
DESIGNERS	Daniel Tang, Wayne Wright
CLIENT	Glen Ellen Carneros Winery
TOOLS	Adobe Photoshop, Macintosh

DESIGN FIRM	Insight Design Communications
ART DIRECTORS	Sherrie & Tracy Holdeman
DESIGNERS	Sherrie & Tracy Holdeman
CLIENT	Richard Lynn's Shoe Market
TOOL	Macromedia FreeHand 9.0.1

DESIGN FIRM	Insight Design Communications
ART DIRECTORS	Sherrie & Tracy Holdeman
DESIGNERS	Sherrie & Tracy Holdeman
CLIENT	Dino's Italian Grille
TOOLS	Hand Drawn, Macromedia FreeHand 9.0.1

DESIGN FIRM	Insight Design Communications
ART DIRECTORS	Sherrie & Tracy Holdeman
DESIGNERS	Sherrie & Tracy Holdeman
CLIENT	Perfect Pitch Sound Systems
TOOLS	Hand Drawn, Macromedia FreeHand 9.0.1

DESIGN FIRM	Insight Design Communications
ART DIRECTORS	Sherrie & Tracy Holdeman
DESIGNERS	Sherrie & Tracy Holdeman
CLIENT	Le Petit Chef
TOOLS	Hand Drawn, Macromedia FreeHand 9.0.1

DESIGN FIRM	Karacters Design Group
ART DIRECTORS	Maria Kennedy, Roy White
DESIGNER	Matthew Clark
CLIENT	Overwaitea Food Group Urban Fare
TOOL	Adobe Illustrator

DESIGN FIRM	Jeff Fisher LogoMotives
ART DIRECTOR	Jeff Fisher
DESIGNER	Jeff Fisher
CLIENT	W.C. Winks Hardware
TOOLS	Macromedia FreeHand, Macintosh

DESIGN FIRM	Jeff Fisher LogoMotives
ART DIRECTOR	Jeff Fisher
DESIGNER	Jeff Fisher
CLIENT	Peggy Sundays
TOOLS	Macromedia FreeHand, Macintosh

DESIGN FIRM	Lloyds Graphic Design & Communication
ART DIRECTOR	Alexander Lloyd
DESIGNER	Alexander Lloyd
CLIENT	One Skinny Cook
TOOLS	Macromedia FreeHand, Macintosh

DESIGN FIRM	Lloyds Graphic Design & Communication
ART DIRECTOR	Alexander Lloyd
DESIGNER	Alexander Lloyd
CLIENT	A Cappella Furniture
TOOLS	Macromedia FreeHand, Macintosh

DESIGN FIRM	Louey/Rubino Design Group
ART DIRECTOR	Robert Louey
CREATIVE DIRECTOR	Tony Chi & Associates
DESIGNER	Alex Chao
CLIENT	NoMi
TOOLS	Quark XPress, Adobe Illustrator, Macintosh

800 NORTH MICHIGAN AVENUE
CHICAGO, ILLINOIS 60611
312 239 4030 T
312 239 4000 F

DESIGN FIRM	Love Communications
ART DIRECTOR	Preston Wood
CLIENT	Orchard Street Market
TOOLS	Adobe Illustrator, Quark XPress

DESIGN FIRM	Total Creative
ART DIRECTOR	Rod Dyer
DESIGNER	Michael Doret
CLIENT	Hollywood & Vine Diner
TOOL	Adobe Illustrator 8.01

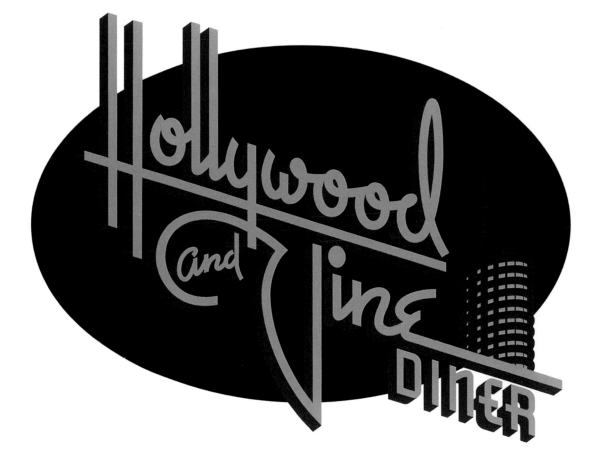

ENGFER PIZZA WORKS

WOOD-FIRED

DESIGN FIRM	Energy Energy Design
ART DIRECTOR	Leslie Guidice
SENIOR DESIGNER	Stacy Guidice
ILLUSTRATOR	Tim Harris
CLIENT	Engfer Pizza Works
TOOLS	Adobe Illustrator, Macintosh

urban feast

DESIGN FIRM	Nesnadny + Schwartz
ART DIRECTOR	Joyce Nesnadny
DESIGNERS	Joyce Nesnadny, Cindy Lowrey
CLIENT	Urban Feast
TOOLS	Macromedia FreeHand 8.0, Macintosh

DESIGN FIRM	Oliver Russell & Associates
ART DIRECTOR	Kristy Weyhrich
DESIGNER	Kristy Weyhrich
CLIENT	Alan Head, Grove Street Place
TOOLS	Adobe Illustrator 8.0, Macintosh G4

DESIGN FIRM | PM Design
ART DIRECTOR | Philip Marzo
DESIGNER | Philip Marzo
CLIENT | B. Heaven.
TOOL | Adobe Illustrator 8.0

HEAVEN

DESIGN FIRM	Palmquist Creative
ART DIRECTOR	Andrea Stevenson
DESIGNER	Kelly Bellcour
CLIENT	Big Sky Carvers–Single Green Frog
TOOLS	Adobe Illustrator, Macintosh

DESIGN FIRM	Shamlian Advertising
ART DIRECTOR	Fred Shamlian
DESIGNERS	Darren Taylor, Edgar Uy
CLIENT	Du Jour Catering
TOOLS	Macintosh, Adobe Illustrator 8.0, Quark XPress 4.1

du j·o·ur
market / catering / patisserie

du j·o·ur
market / catering / patisserie

sally walsh proprietor
haverford square 379 lancaster ave. haverford, PA 19041
tel. 610.896.4556 **fax** 610.896.5944

du j·o·ur
market / catering / patisserie

haverford square
379 lancaster ave.
haverford, PA 19041

du jour **market/catering/patisserie** haverford square 379 lancaster ave. haverford, PA 19041 **tel.** 610.896.4556 **fax** 610.896.5944

DESIGN FIRM	Second Floor
ART DIRECTOR	Warren Welter
DESIGNER	Chris Twilling
CLIENT	Personality Hotels
TOOLS	Adobe Illustrator, Quark XPress, Macintosh

DESIGN FIRM | Lewis Moberly
ART DIRECTOR | Mary Lewis
DESIGNER | Joanne Smith
CLIENT | Finca Flichman
TOOL | Adobe Illustrator8.0, Macintosh

FINCA FLICHMAN

WINERY

DESIGN FIRM	Sayles Graphic Design
ART DIRECTOR	John Sayles
DESIGNER	John Sayles
CLIENT	Sayles Graphic Design
TOOLS	Adobe Illustrator, Macintosh

DESIGN FIRM	Sonsoles Llorens
ART DIRECTOR	Sonsoles Llorens
DESIGNER	Sonsoles Llorens
CLIENT	Storage/Marta Sanllehi, Javier Crosas
TOOLS	Macromedia FreeHand, Macintosh

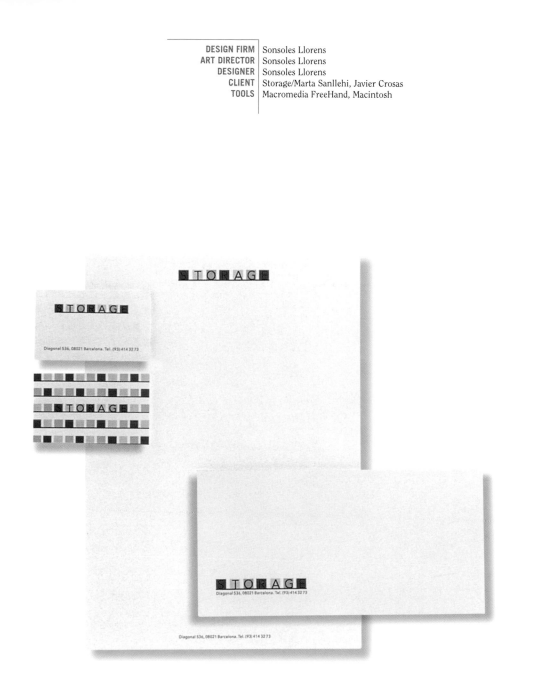

DESIGN FIRM	Sonsoles Llorens
ART DIRECTOR	Sonsoles Llorens
DESIGNER	Sonsoles Llorens
CLIENT	Publicentre S.A./Enric Vives, Chairman
TOOLS	Macromedia FreeHand, Adobe Photoshop, Streamline, Macintosh

1 NESNADNY + SCHWARTZ | ART DIRECTOR JOYCE NESNADNY | DESIGNER MICHELLE MOEHLER | CLIENT SMART PAPERS

1

2

3

1 HONEY DESIGN | ART DIRECTOR ROBIN HONEY | CLIENT TWO PAWS UP

2 SAYLES GRAPHIC DESIGN | DESIGNER JOHN SAYLES | CLIENT BUSY BEE TAILORING

3 SAYLES GRAPHIC DESIGN | ART DIRECTOR JOHN SAYLES | CLIENT CLOUD 9

1

2

1 **PURE DESIGN INC.** | ART DIRECTOR **RACHELLE FISHER** | DESIGNER **JOHN FISHER** | CLIENT **IDYLWILDE FLIES**

2 **GILLESPIE DESIGN INC.** | ART DIRECTOR **MAUREEN GILLESPIE** | DESIGNER **LIZ SCHENKEL** | CLIENT **WENDY AND AMY (BABY STATIONERY)**

ENERGY ENERGY DESIGN | ART DIRECTOR LESLIE GUIDICE | DESIGNERS STACY GUIDICE, JEANETTE ARAMBURU | CLIENT ACME CHOPHOUSE

1

2

3

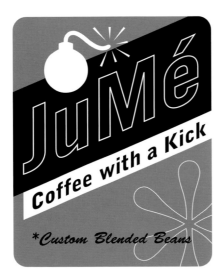

4

ORIGINAL CASUAL APPAREL FOR FENCERS

CAHOOTS | ART DIRECTOR CAROL LASKEY | DESIGNER JOHN HOFSTETTER | CLIENT BIG FOR OUR BRITCHES

1

2

3

1 **PUBLICIDAD GÓMEZ CHICA** | DESIGNER **SANTIAGO JARAMILLO** | CLIENT **LAS PALMAS RESTAURANT**
2 **SAYLES GRAPHIC DESIGN** | ART DIRECTOR **JOHN SAYLES** | CLIENT **PETALS DE PROVENCE**
3 **SAYLES GRAPHIC DESIGN** | DESIGNER **JOHN SAYLES** | CLIENT **NEPTUNE'S SEAGRILL**

1

2

1 BE.DESIGN | ART DIRECTOR WILL BURKE | DESIGNERS ERIC READ, YUSUKE ASAKA, CORALIE RUSSO | CLIENT WORLDWISE, INC.

2 RE: SALZMAN DESIGNS | ART DIRECTOR IDA CHEINMAN | DESIGNERS IDA CHEINMAN, RICK SALZMAN | CLIENT LEE'S ICE CREAM

1

2

3

4

1 **HG DESIGN** | DESIGNER **MATT PIERCE** | CLIENT **THUNDER EAGLE CYCLE SHOP**
2 **CFX CREATIVE** | ART DIRECTOR **CARLY H. FRANKLIN** | CLIENT **MEDBIZMARKET**
3 **GASKET** | ART DIRECTOR **MIKE CHRISTOFFEL** | CLIENT **GLAM**
4 **RICK JOHNSON & COMPANY** | DESIGNER **TIM MCGRATH** | CLIENT **CRUSTY UNDERWEAR**

Custodians of fine Australian wine

WOOL
LOO
MOO
WINES LOO

David Titsha
General Manager

Telephone +61 2 9252 0080
Facsimile +61 2 9252 8878

Woolloomooloo Wines
Royal Exchange PO Box R384
Sydney 1225 NSW
Australia

david@woolloomooloowines.com.au
www.woolloomooloowines.com.au

Custodians of fine Australian wine

WOOL
LOO
MOO
WINES LOO

ine Australian wine

WOOL
LOO
MOO
WINES LOO

Woolloomooloo
pron. wool-lōō-mōō-lōō

The name Woolloomooloo is
steeped in indigenous Australian
[Aboriginal] heritage. The name
originally comes from 'Wulla Nulla'
meaning 'young male kangaroo'.

WOOL
LOO
MOO
WINES LOO

Telephone +61 2 9252 0080
Facsimile +61 2 9252 8878

Woolloomooloo Wines Pty Limited
Royal Exchange PO Box R384
Sydney 1225 NSW Australia

www.woolloomooloowines.com.au
ABN 26 080 837 084

John Olsen

EMERY VINCENT DESIGN | ART DIRECTOR EMERY VINCENT DESIGN | CLIENT WOOLLOOMOOLOO WINES

1

SLAVE

2

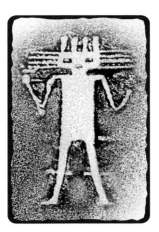

ATACAMA

1 BE.DESIGN | ART DIRECTOR ERIC READ | DESIGNER DEBORAH SMITH READ | CLIENT SLAVE
2 BE.DESIGN | ART DIRECTOR ERIC READ | DESIGNERS ERIC READ, CORALIE RUSSO | CLIENT COST PLUS WORLD MARKET

Harrods
KNIGHTSBRIDGE

URBAN RETREAT AT HARRODS
Fifth Floor, Harrods, Knightsbridge London SW1X 7XL Telephone 020 7893 8333 Fax 020 7893 8335
Registered in England No 2849316 VAT No 627575022 Registered Office Urban Retreats Limited 7 Munton Road London SE17 1PR

D. DESIGN | ART DIRECTOR DEREK SAMUEL | CLIENT GEORGE HAMMER

1

2

3

1 BAKKEN CREATIVE CO. | ART DIRECTOR MICHELLE BAKKEN | CLIENT FRASCATI RESTAURANT
2 BE.DESIGN | ART DIRECTOR WILL BURKE | DESIGNERS ERIC READ, DIANE HILDE | CLIENT COST PLUS WORLD MARKET
3 METZLER ASSOCIATES | ART DIRECTOR MARC-ANTOINE HERRMANN | DESIGNER JEAN-RENEE GUEGAN | CLIENT SCAPPUCCI

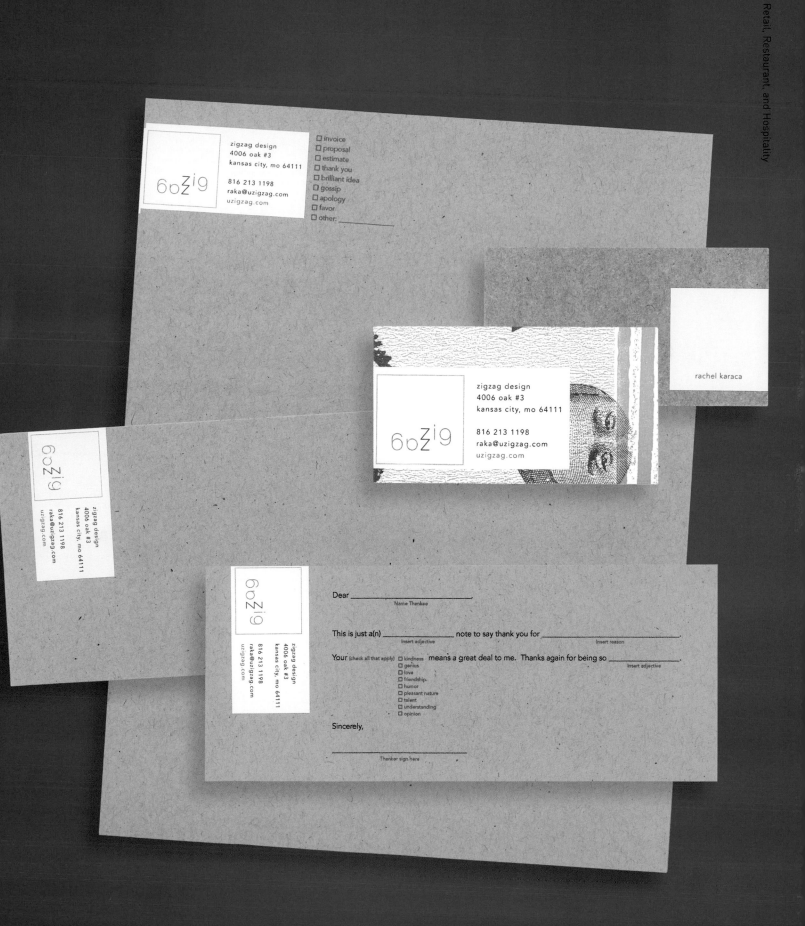

taktil.

taktil.

Dirk Wallstein
Geschäftsführung

Gesellschaft für
Kommunikation bR mbH

Hedwigstr. 24
D-44809 Bochum
Fon   +49 (0) 2 34 • 95 71 94-13
Fax   +49 (0) 2 34 • 95 71 94-99
mobil   +49 (0) 1 63 • 3 10 47 13
email   wallstein@taktil.de
Internet www.taktil.de

GRAPHISCHE FORMGEBUNG | ART DIRECTOR HERBERT ROHSIEPE | CLIENT TAKTIL. GESELLSCHAFT FÜR KOMMUNIKATION

Chapter 4:

RECREATION AND ENTERTAINMENT

design firm | **Mires Design**
art director | **John Ball**
designers | **John Ball, Miguel Perez**
illustrator | **Tracy Sabin**
client | **Nike Inc.**

design firm | **Mires Design**
art director | **John Ball**
designers | **John Ball, Deborah Horn**
client | **Nike, Inc.**

design firm | **DogStar Design**
art director | **Jennifer Martin**
designer | **Jennifer Martin**
client | **Roaring Tiger Films**
tool | **Macromedia FreeHand**

design firm	**The Riordon Design Group, Inc.**
art director	**Ric Riordon**
designers	**Dan Wheaton, Sharon Porter**
client	**Free TV**
tools	**Adobe Illustrator, Quark XPress, Adobe Photoshop**
paper/printing	**Bravo/Contact Creative**

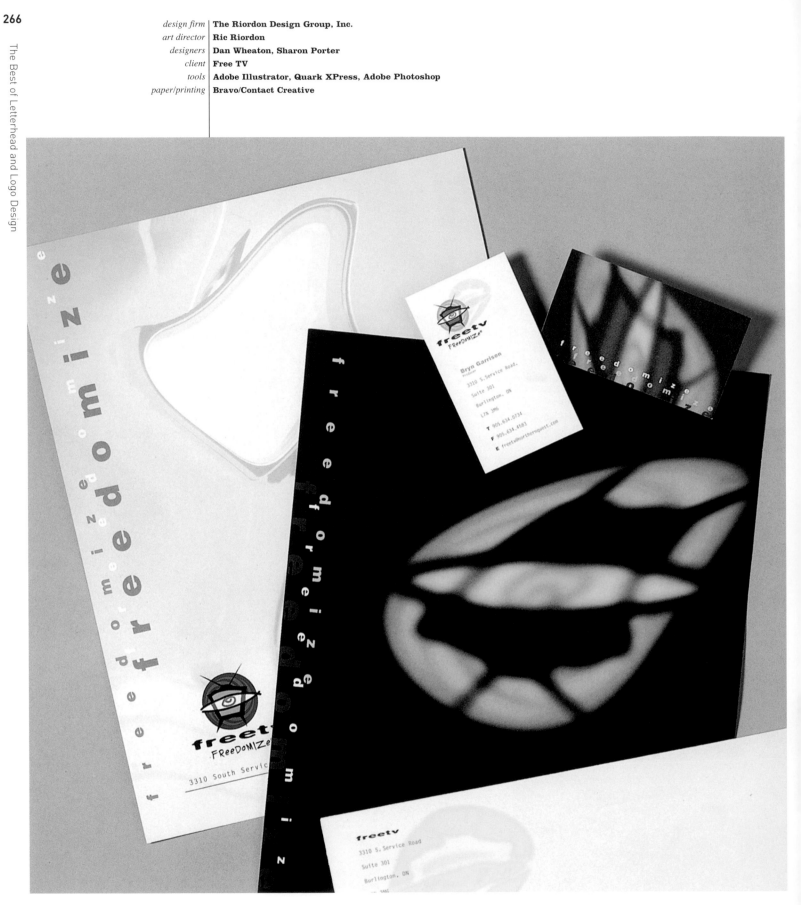

design firm	**Iron Design**
art director	**Todd Edmonds**
designer	**Jim Keller**
client	**Ripcord Games**
tool	**Adobe Illustrator**
paper/printing	**Strathmore/Four-color process, metallic silver**

Henry Moyer
National Sales Manager,
Audio

88 Saint Francis St
Newark NJ 07105

973.344.4214
973.344.2233 Fax

www.peterpan.com

PPI Entertainment

PPI Entertainment

design firm	**Iron Design**
art director	**Todd Edmonds**
designer	**Ted Skibinski**
client	**PPI Entertainment**
tools	**Adobe Dimensions, Adobe Illustrator**
paper/printing	**Mohawk/Four-color process, metallic silver**

design firm	Mires Design
art director	Jose Serrano
designers	Jose Serrano, Miguel Perez
client	Hell Racer

design firm	Mires Design
art director	Jose Serrano
designers	Jose Serrano, Miguel Perez
client	Hell Racer

design firm | **Art Chantry Design Company**
designer | **Art Chantry**
client | **Estrus Records**

design firm | **Art Chantry Design Company**
designer | **Art Chantry**
client | **Hell's Elevator Productions**

design firm	**Jim Lange Design**
art director	**Jan Caille**
designer	**Jim Lange**
client	**Mrs. T's Chicago Triathlon**
tools	**Macintosh, Hand illustration**
paper/printing	**Smith Printing**

design firm	**Sametz Blackstone Associates**
art director	**Robert Beerman**
designe	**Hania Khuri**
client	**90.9 WBUR/The Connection**
tools	**Quark XPress, Adobe Photoshop, Macintosh Power PC**
paper/printing	**24 lb. Strathmore Writing Bright White/Puritan Press**

M·C·A
MUSIC CORPORATION
of AMERICA

70 UNIVERSAL CITY PLAZA   UNIVERSAL CITY, CALIFORNIA   USA   91608   818.777.4000 T   WWW.MCARECORDS.COM

design firm	**Segura, Inc.**
art director	**Carlos Segura**
designers	**Carlos Segura,**
	Susana Detembleque
client	**MCA**
tools	**Adobe Photoshop, Adobe Illustrator**

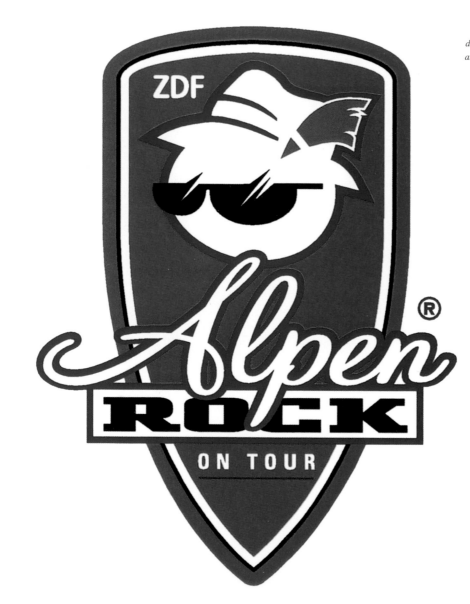

design firm | **Simon & Goetz Design**
art director | **Ruediger Goetz**
designer | **Ruediger Goetz**
illustrator | **Manuela Schmidt**
client | **ZDF**

DESIGN FIRM	Anderson Thomas Design
ART DIRECTORS	Jay Smith, Joel Anderson
DESIGNER	Jay Smith
CLIENT	The Nashville Symphony
TOOLS	Adobe Illustrator, Macintosh

THE NASHVILLE SYMPHONY

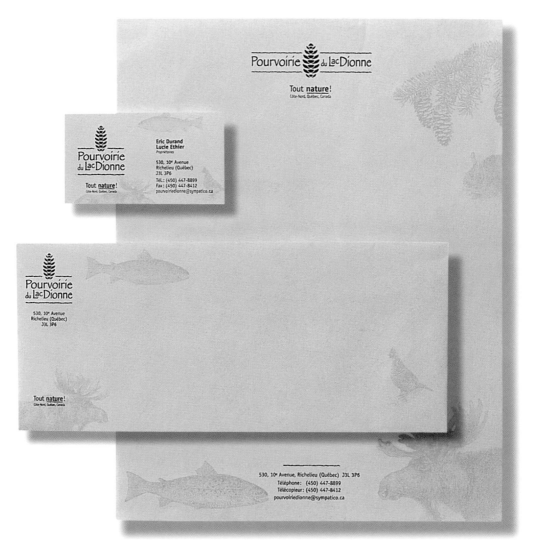

DESIGN FIRM	Beaulieu Concepts Graphiques, Inc.
ART DIRECTOR	Gilles Beaulieu
DESIGNER	Gilles Beaulieu
CLIENT	Pourvoirie du Lac Dionne
TOOLS	Adobe Photoshop, Adobe Illustrator, Macintosh

DESIGN FIRM	Cato Partners
DESIGNER	Cato Partners
CLIENT	Melbourne International Festival of the Arts
TOOLS	Adobe Illustrator 6, Macintosh

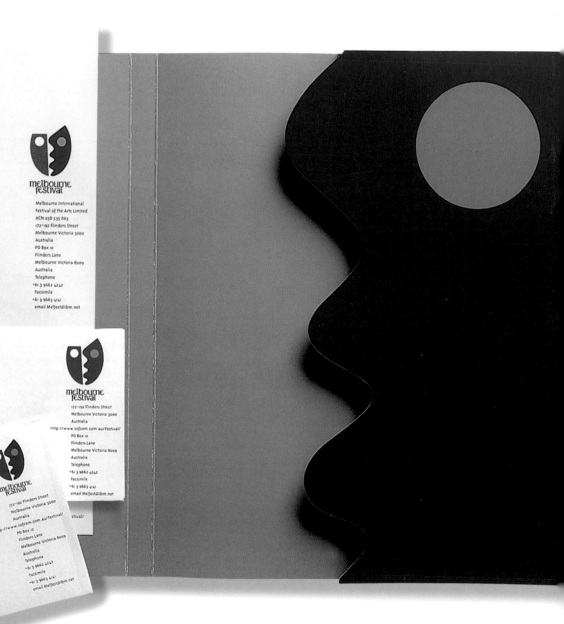

WELLSPRING

DESIGN FIRM | Design Center
ART DIRECTOR | John Reger
DESIGNER | Sherwin Schwartzrock
CLIENT | Wellspring
TOOLS | Macromedia FreeHand, Macintosh

DESIGN FIRM	C.W.A., Inc.
ART DIRECTOR	Calvin Woo
DESIGNER	Marco Sipriaso
CLIENT	Asian-American Journalists
	Association/San Diego Asian Film Festival
TOOL	Adobe Illustrator 9

TRANQUILLITY

TRANQUILLITY

Larry Barnet Captain

Telephone 871 32 531 4910
Facsimile 871 32 531 4911

Telephone 871 32 531 4910   *Facsimile* 871 32 531 4911

DESIGN FIRM	Drive Communications
ART DIRECTOR	Michael Graziolo
DESIGNER	Michael Graziolo
CLIENT	Michael Bloomberg/Tranquility
TOOLS	Adobe Illustrator 8.0, Macintosh

DESIGN FIRM	Duarte Design
ART DIRECTOR	Dave Zavala
DESIGNER	Dave Zavala
CLIENT	Cubìco
TOOLS	Adobe Illustrator, Quark XPress, Adobe Photoshop, Macintosh

DESIGN FIRM	Gardner Design
ART DIRECTORS	Travis Brown, Bill Gardner
DESIGNER	Travis Brown
CLIENT	The Oaks
TOOLS	Macromedia FreeHand, Adobe Photoshop

DESIGN FIRM	Hornall Anderson Design Works, Inc.
ART DIRECTOR	Jack Anderson
DESIGNERS	Jack Anderson, Andrew Smith, Mary Chin Hutchison, Taro Sakita
CLIENT	K2 Corporation/K2 Skis Mod Logo
TOOL	Adobe Photoshop

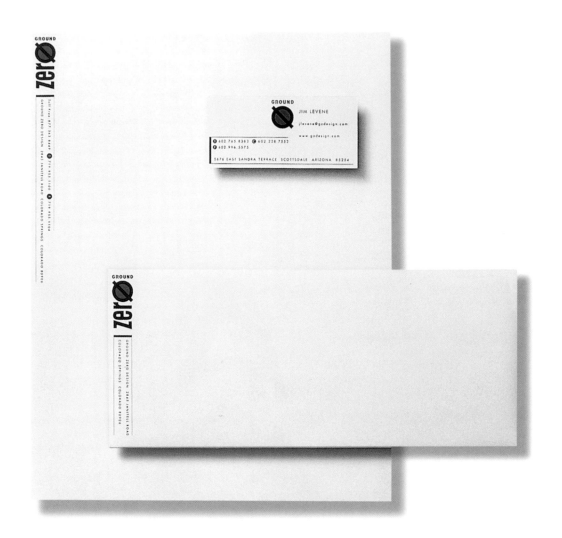

DESIGN FIRM	Hornall Anderson Design Works, Inc.
ART DIRECTOR	Jack Anderson
DESIGNERS	Jack Anderson, Kathy Saito, Julie Lock, Ed Lee, Heidi Favour, Virginia Le, Sonja Max
CLIENT	Ground Zero
TOOL	Macromedia FreeHand

DESIGN FIRM	Hornall Anderson Design Works, Inc.
ART DIRECTOR	Jack Anderson
DESIGNERS	Jack Anderson, Belinda Bowling, Andrew Smith, Don Stayner
CLIENT	Streamworks
TOOL	Adobe Illustrator

STREAMWORKS

STREAMWORKS

STREAMWORKS

NAME | TITLE
Bob Caldwell | Chairman & President
STREET | SUITE | CITY | STATE | ZIP CODE
1500 Westlake Ave. N. | 118 | Seattle | WA | 98109-3036
PHONE | FAX | TOLL FREE
206.301.9292 | 206.378.1438 | 800.611.0008
EMAIL | INTERNET
bobca@streamworks.org | www.streamworks.org

PHONE | FAX | INTERNET | STREET | SUITE | CITY | STATE | ZIP CODE
206.301.9292 | 206.378.1438 | www.streamworks.org | 1500 Westlake Ave N | 118 | Seattle | WA | 98109

DESIGN FIRM	Hornall Anderson Design Works, Inc.
ART DIRECTOR	Jack Anderson
DESIGNERS	Jack Anderson, Katha Dalton, Henry Yiu, Tiffany Scheiblauer, Darlin Gray, Brad Sherman
CLIENT	Recharge
TOOL	Macromedia FreeHand

DESIGN FIRM | Insight Design Communications
ART DIRECTORS | Sherrie & Tracy Holdeman
DESIGNERS | Sherrie & Tracy Holdeman
CLIENT | 4Points Travel
TOOLS | Hand Drawn, Macromedia FreeHand 9.0.1

DESIGN FIRM	Jeff Fisher LogoMotives
ART DIRECTOR	Jeff Fisher
DESIGNER	Jeff Fisher
CLIENT	Triangle Productions!
TOOLS	Macromedia FreeHand, Macintosh

DESIGN FIRM	Lloyds Graphic Design & Communication
ART DIRECTOR	Alexander Lloyd
DESIGNER	Alexander Lloyd
CLIENT	Functions Unlimited
TOOLS	Macromedia FreeHand, Macintosh

TOTAL EVENT DIRECTION

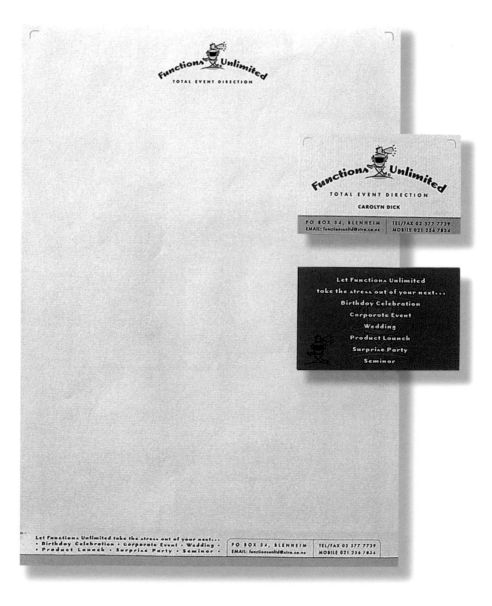

DESIGN FIRM	Michael Doret Graphic Design
ART DIRECTOR	Joel Hladecek
DESIGNER	Michael Doret
CLIENT	Red Sky Interactive
TOOL	Adobe Illustrator 8.01

E A S T   T O W E R

S O U T H   T O W E R

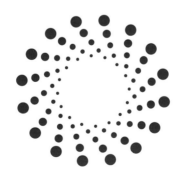

N O R T H   T O W E R

GOTTSCHALK + ASH INTERNATIONAL | ART DIRECTOR STUART ASH | DESIGNER SONJA CHOW | CLIENT BELL MOBILITY OFFICES

1

2

1 **CHASE DESIGN GROUP** | ART DIRECTOR **MARGO CHASE** | CLIENT **THE WB TV NETWORK**
2 **CHASE DESIGN GROUP** | ART DIRECTOR **MARGO CHASE** | CLIENT **THE WB TV NETWORK**

1 **I. PARIS DESIGN** | ART DIRECTOR **ISAAC PARIS** | CLIENT **RECORD TIME LABEL**

2 **PACEY + PACEY** | ART DIRECTOR **ROBERT PACEY** | DESIGNER **MICHAEL PACEY** | CLIENT **VANCOUVER DART ASSOC.**

3 **SAGMEISTER INC.** | ART DIRECTOR **STEFAN SAGMEISTER** | DESIGNER **MATHIAS ERNSTBERGER** | CLIENT **LOU REED**

Chapter 5:

EDUCATION, HEALTH, AND NONPROFIT

design firm	**Sayles Graphic Design**
art director	**John Sayles**
designer	**John Sayles**
client	**Goodtime Jazz Festival**
tool	**Macintosh**
paper/printing	**Neenah Bond/Offset**

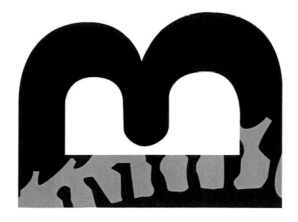

BOCATRIOL®
calcitriol

design firm | **Leo Pharmaceutical Products**
art director | **Martin Isbrand**
designer | **Martin Isbrand**
client | **Leo Pharmaceutical Products**

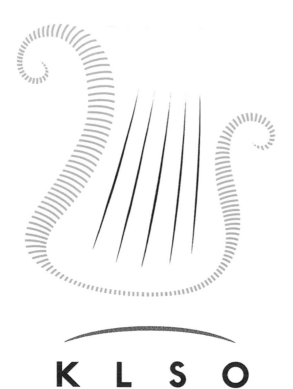

K L S O

design firm | **Werk-Haus**
designers | **Ezrah Rahim, Paggie Chin Lee Choo**
client | **Kuala Lumpur Symphony Orchestra Society**
tool | **Macintosh**

design firm	Patricia Bruning Design
art director	Patricia Bruning
designers	Patricia Bruning, Fran Terry
client	Seven Tepees Youth Program
tools	Quark XPress 3.32, Adobe Illustrator 6.0, Macintosh 7100 Power PC
paper/printing	Hamilton Press

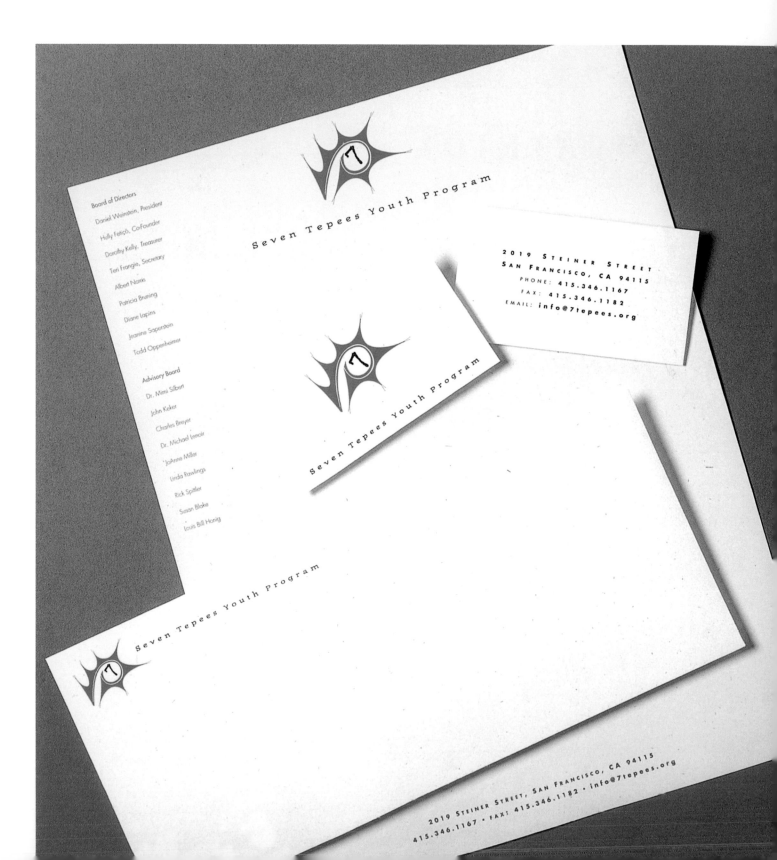

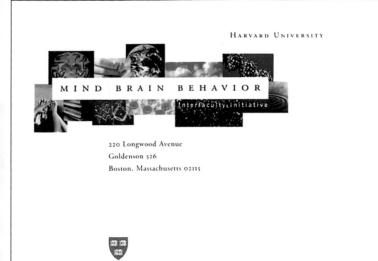

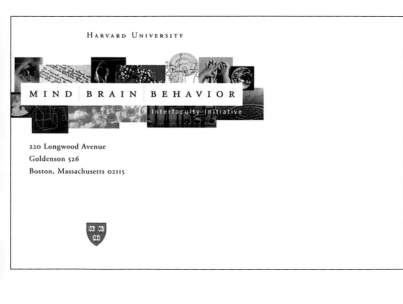

design firm	**Visual Dialogue**
art director	**Fritz Klaetke**
designers	**Fritz Klaetke, David Kraljic**
client	**Harvard University**
tools	**Quark XPress, Adobe Photoshop, Macintosh Power PC**
paper/printing	**Strathmore Elements/Color Express**

design firm	**The Point Group**
designer	**David Howard**
client	**Big Brothers & Big Sisters of Dallas**
tool	**Adobe Illustrator**

design firm	**Leo Pharmaceutical Products**
art director	**Martin Isbrand**
designer	**Martin Isbrand**
client	**Leo Pharmaceutical Products**

design firm	**Vanderbyl Design**
art director	**Michael Vanderbyl**
designers	**Michael Vanderbyl, Erica ,Wilcott**
client	**The American Center for Wine, Food & the Arts**
tools	**Quark XPress, Adobe Illustrator**
paper/printing	**Cranes Crest/Trade Engraving**

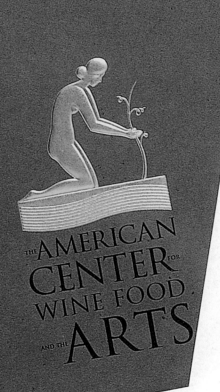

PEGGY A. LOAR
DIRECTOR

FRANCES A. ANAMOSA
EXECUTIVE ASSISTANT
1700 SOSCOL AVE SUITE I NAPA CA 94559
TEL 707·257·3606 FAX 707·257·8601
EMAIL: fanamosa@theamericancenter.org

304

design firm	**Sayles Graphic Design**
art director	**John Sayles**
designer	**John Sayles**
client	**Sue Roberts Health Concepts**
tool	**Macintosh**
paper/printing	**Neenah Environment Natural/Four-color offset**

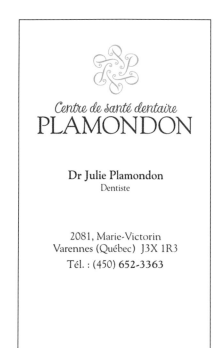

Centre de santé dentaire
PLAMONDON

Dr Julie Plamondon
Dentiste

2081, Marie-Victorin
Varennes (Québec) J3X 1R3
Tél. : (450) **652-3363**

DESIGN FIRM	Beaulieu Concepts Graphiques, Inc.
ART DIRECTOR	Gilles Beaulieu
DESIGNER	Gilles Beaulieu
CLIENT	Dr. Julie Plamondon
TOOLS	Adobe Photoshop, Adobe Illustrator, Macintosh

DESIGN FIRM	Bakker Design
ART DIRECTOR	Doug Bakker
DESIGNERS	Doug Bakker, Brian Sauer
CLIENT	Mentor Iowa
TOOLS	Macromedia FreeHand 9, Macintosh

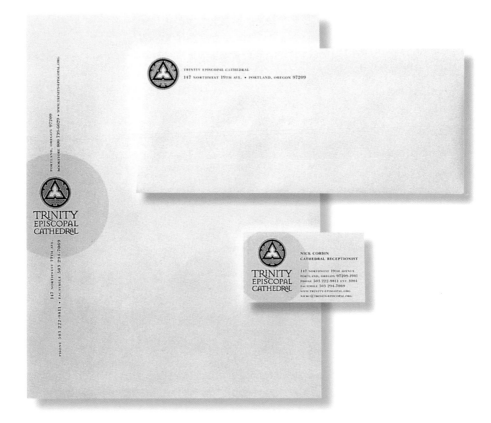

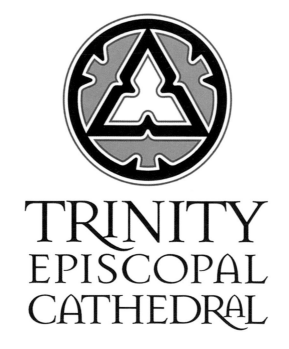

DESIGN FIRM	Bailey/Franklin
ART DIRECTOR	Connie Lightner
DESIGNER	Connie Lightner
CLIENT	Trinity Episcopal Cathedral
TOOLS	Quark XPress, Adobe Illustrator, Macintosh

DESIGN FIRM	Design Center
ART DIRECTOR	John Reger
DESIGNER	Sherwin Schwartzrock
CLIENT	Minnesota School Boards Association
TOOLS	Macromedia FreeHand, Macintosh

DESIGN FIRM	Hornall Anderson Design Works, Inc.
ART DIRECTORS	Jack Anderson, Lisa Cerveny
DESIGNERS	Lisa Cerveny, Jana Nishi, Bruce Branson-Meyer, Don Stayner, Mary Chin Hutchison, Jack Anderson
CLIENT	XOW!
TOOL	Macromedia FreeHand

THE
MCDOUGAL CENTER

BLUE DOG
CAFE

DESIGN FIRM	Icehouse Design
ART DIRECTOR	Bjorn Akselsen
DESIGNER	Bjorn Akselsen
CLIENT	Yale University's Blue Dog Café
TOOLS	Adobe Illustrator, Macintosh

ART DIRECTOR | Melanie Sherwood
DESIGNER | Melanie Sherwood
CLIENT | Unity Center of Positive Prayer
TOOLS | Adobe Illustrator, Macintosh

UNITY CENTER

A CHURCH OF POSITIVE PRAYER

DESIGN FIRM | Miriello Grafico
ART DIRECTOR | Chris Keeney
DESIGNER | Chris Keeney
CLIENT | Visser
TOOL | Adobe Illustrator

The Best of Letterhead and Logo Design

DESIGN FIRM	Stoltze Design
ART DIRECTOR	Clifford Stoltze
DESIGNERS	Lee Schulz, Cindy Patten, Brandon Blangger
CLIENT	Six Red Marbles
TOOLS	Macromedia FreeHand, Adobe Illustrator, Quark XPress, Macintosh

DESIGN FIRM	Sayles Graphic Design
ART DIRECTOR	John Sayles
DESIGNER	John Sayles
CLIENT	Advertising Professionals of Des Moines
TOOLS	Adobe Illustrator, Macintosh

DESIGN FIRM	Stewart Monderer Design, Inc.
ART DIRECTOR	Stewart Monderer
DESIGNERS	Jeffrey Gobin, Stewart Monderer
CLIENT	Massachusetts Bar Association
TOOLS	Adobe Illustrator, Quark XPress, Macintosh

1

2

3

1 **DUO DESIGN** | DESIGNERS **VALTERS LINDBERGS, EMMANUELLE BECKER** | CLIENT **FRANCE TELECOM FORMATION**

2 **LEAGAS DELANEY SF** | DESIGNER **EMILIA FILIPOI** | CLIENT **STEP UP NETWORK**

3 **HONEY DESIGN** | ART DIRECTOR **ROBIN HONEY** | DESIGNER **JASON RECKER** | CLIENT **CALLAGHAN CONSULTING**

1

2

1 GUNNAR SWANSON DESIGN OFFICE | ART DIRECTOR GUNNAR SWANSON | CLIENT CALIFORNIA STATE POLYTECHNIC UNIVERSITY
2 I, PARIS DESIGN | ART DIRECTOR ISAAC PARIS | CLIENT NATURAL GAS VEHICLES

T D C T J H T B I P C

T D C T J H T B I P C

the redoubtable potentate
MR. THARP
phone 408.354.6726 *fax* 408.354.1450

50 UNIVERSITY AVE., LOFT 21 │ LOS GATOS, CA 95030 │ WWW.TDCTJHTBIPC.ORG

1

2

3

1 FRESHBRAND, INC. | ART DIRECTOR MARCEL VENTER | CLIENT CREATIVE ADOPTIONS
2 GOTT FOLK MCCANN-ERIKSON | ART DIRECTOR EINRA GYLFAYSON | CLIENT MENNT.IS
3 ALR DESIGN | ART DIRECTOR NOAH SCALIN | CLIENT ABC NO RIO

URBAN HABITAT

URBAN HABITAT

JULIET ELLIS
EXECUTIVE DIRECTOR

436 14TH STREET, STE 1205
OAKLAND, CA 94612
T 510 839 9512 F 510 839 9610
jre@urbanhabitat.org
www.urbanhabitat.org

URBAN HABITAT

436 14TH STREET, STE 1205
OAKLAND, CA 94612

436 14TH STREET, STE 1205   OAKLAND, CA 94612
T 510 839 9510 F 510 839 9610
www.urbanhabitat.org

TOM & JOHN: ADC | ART DIRECTOR TOM SIEU | CLIENT URBAN HABITAT

Science Council of British Columbia

Helping

Make

Tomorrow

Happen

in BC

Science Council of British Columbia

Suite 800

4710 Kingsway

Burnaby

British Columbia

Canada V5H 4M2

Telephone

(604) 438-2752

Call Toll Free

1-800-665-SCBC (7222)

Facsimile

(604) 438-6564

PACEY + PACEY | ART DIRECTOR **MICHAEL PACEY** | CLIENT **SCIENCE COUNCIL OF BRITISH COLUMBIA**

1

2

BOOK OF LIFE
Jewish Community Foundation

3

1 **FUSZION COLLABORATIVE** | ART DIRECTOR **JOHN FOSTER** | CLIENT **AMERICANS FOR THE ARTS**
2 **MORRIS CREATIVE INC.** | ART DIRECTOR **STEVEN MORRIS** | DESIGNER **TRACY MEINERS** | CLIENT **JEWISH COMMUNITY FOUNDATION**
3 **SAYLES GRAPHIC DESIGN** | ART DIRECTOR **JOHN SAYLES** | CLIENT **GIRL SCOUTS OF CHICAGO**

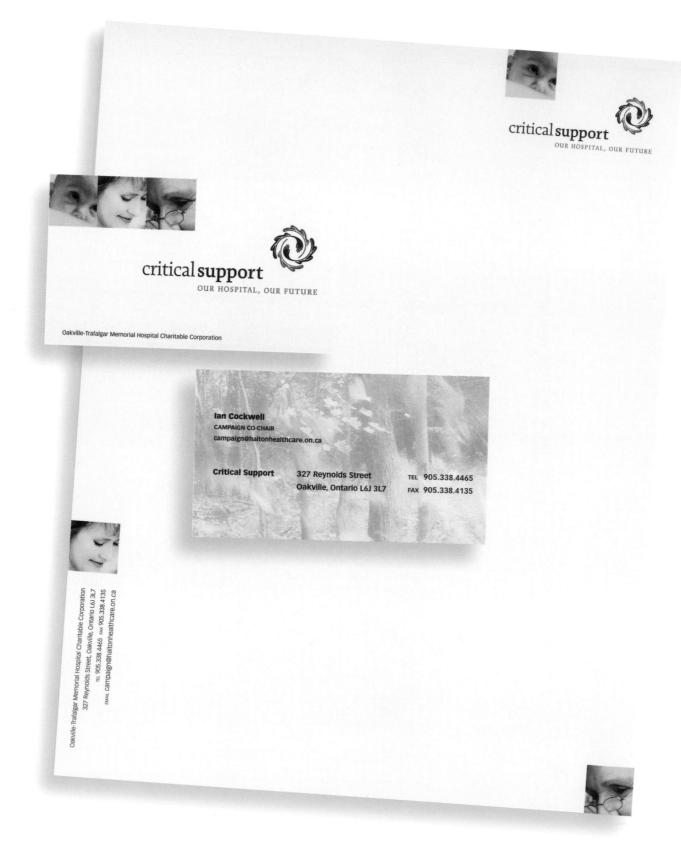

critical support

OUR HOSPITAL, OUR FUTURE

critical support

OUR HOSPITAL, OUR FUTURE

Oakville-Trafalgar Memorial Hospital Charitable Corporation

Ian Cockwell
CAMPAIGN CO-CHAIR
campaign@haltonhealthcare.on.ca

Critical Support   327 Reynolds Street   TEL 905.338.4465
                        Oakville, Ontario L6J 3L7   FAX 905.338.4135

Oakville-Trafalgar Memorial Hospital Charitable Corporation
327 Reynolds Street, Oakville, Ontario L6J 3L7
TEL 905.338.4465 FAX 905.338.4135
EMAIL campaign@haltonhealthcare.on.ca

THE RIORDON DESIGN GROUP | ART DIRECTOR DAN WHFATON | DESIGNER ALAN KPPAN | CLIENT OAKVILLE-TRAFALGAR MEMORIAL HOSPITAL

Chapter 6:

MISCELLANEOUS

design firm | **Insight Design Communications**
art directors | **Tracy Holdeman, Sherrie Holdeman**
designers | **Tracy Holdeman, Sherrie Holdeman**
client | **Clotia Wood & Metal Works**
tools | **Macromedia FreeHand 7.0, Macintosh**

design firm	**Synergy Design**
designers	**Leon Alvarado**
client	**Mega Estaclon**
tools	**Macromedia FreeHand,**
	Macintosh
paper/printing	**Various**

design firm	**Murrie Lienhart Rysner**
art director	**Linda Voll**
designer	**Linda Voll**
client	**The Fine Line**
tool	**Adobe Illustrator**

schwer **S** präzision

Schwer Präzision GmbH   Hauptstraße 148   D - 78588 Denkingen

Schwer Präzision GmbH	Telefon	Registergericht Tuttlingen	Kreissparkasse Spaichingen
Drehteile u. Techn. Produkte	07424 / 98 15-0	HRB 571 Sp. Sitz: Denkingen	643 500 70 Kto 455 095
Hauptstraße 148	Fax	Geschäftsführer: Klaus Schwer	Raiffeisenbank Denkingen
D - 78588 Denkingen	07424 / 98 15-30	USt.-Id.-Nr. DE 811731829	643 626 13 Kto 50 444 000

design firm | **revoLUZion**
art director | **Bernd Luz**
designer | **Bernd Luz**
client | **Schwer Präzision**
tools | **Macromedia FreeHand, Macintosh**

design firm	**Russell, Inc.**
art director	**Bob Russell**
client	**Cancom, Inc.**

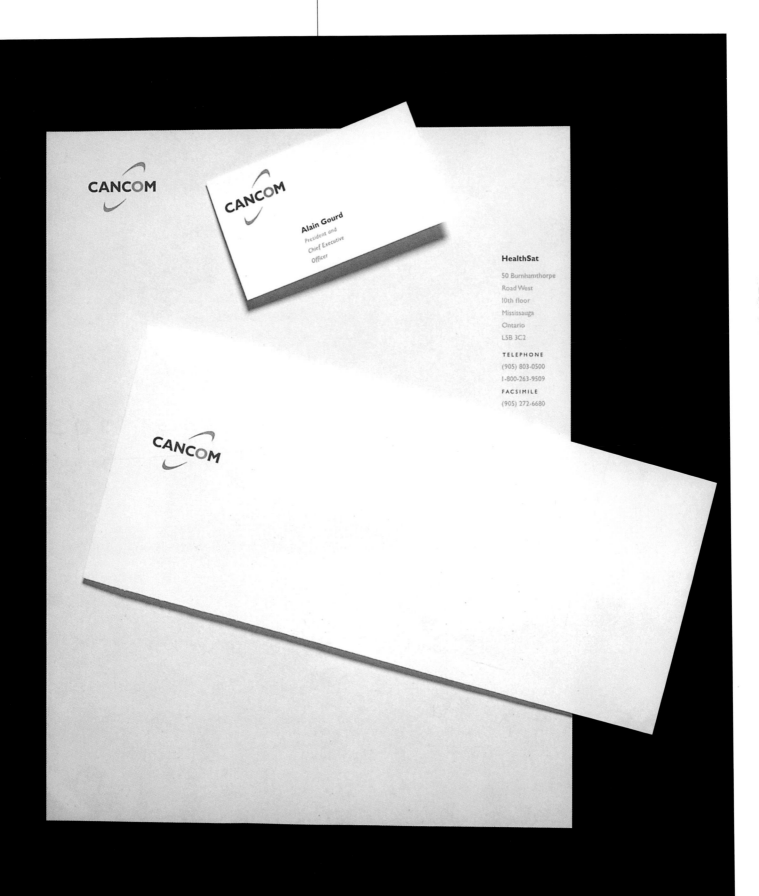

design firm	Segura, Inc.
art director	Carlos Segura
designe	Carlos Segura
client	Blue Rock
tools	Adobe Photoshop, Adobe Illustrator

design firm	**Slover and Company**
art director	**Susan Slover**
designer	**Tamara Behar**
client	**Robert Allen Contract Fabrics**
tools	**Adobe Illustrator, Quark XPress,**
	Macintosh Power PC
paper/printing	**Two-color offset**

design firm	**Patricia Bruning Design**
art director	**Patricia Bruning**
designers	**Patricia Bruning, Fran Terry**
client	**Johnson Hoke**
tools	**Quark XPress 3.32, Adobe Illustrator 6.0,**
	Macintosh 7100 Power PC
paper/printing	**Golden Dragon Printing**

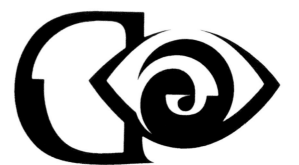

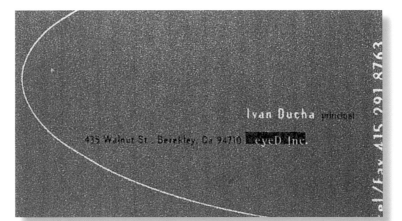

design firm	**Cynthia Patten**
art director	**Cynthia Patten**
designer	**Cynthia Patten**
client	**Eye D**
tools	**Quark XPress 3.32, Adobe Illustrator 6.0, Macintosh 7100 Power PC**
paper/printing	**French Paper Frostone (Iceberg)/ Epson Ink Jet**

IVR Rohloff An der Schluse 23 D-48329 Havixbeck

Industrie-Vertretung
Rohloff

An der Schluse 23
D-48329 Havixbeck

Tel. 0 25 07 - 44 99
Fax 0 25 07 - 13 05

Vertrieb elektronischer
Geräte und Systeme

design firm	**revoLUZion**
art director	**Bernd Luz**
designer	**Bernd Luz**
client	**IVR Rohloff**
tools	**Macromedia Freehand, Macintosh**

DESIGN FIRM | Anderson Thomas Design
ART DIRECTOR | Joel Anderson
DESIGNER | Ramay Lewis
CLIENT | Hardwear
TOOLS | Adobe Illustrator, Adobe Photoshop, Macintosh

DESIGN FIRM	Buchanan Design
ART DIRECTOR	Bobby Buchanan
DESIGNERS	Armando Abundis, Bobby Buchanan
CLIENT	Hispanicvista.com
TOOLS	Adobe Illustrator, Macintosh

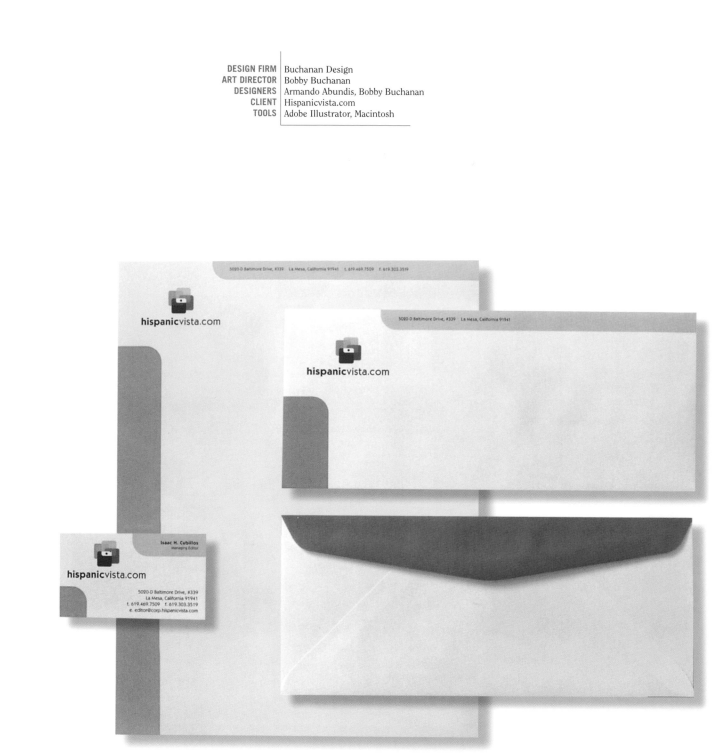

DESIGN FIRM	Catalina Design Group
ART DIRECTOR	Elena Abee
DESIGNER	Elena Abee
CLIENT	D.R. Horton
TOOLS	Adobe Illustrator, Adobe Photoshop

DESIGN FIRM	Catalina Design Group
ART DIRECTOR	Elena Abee
DESIGNER	Elena Abee
CLIENT	Continental
TOOLS	Adobe Illustrator, Adobe Photoshop

DESIGN FIRM	Gardner Design
ART DIRECTOR	Chris Parks
DESIGNER	Chris Parks
CLIENT	Blue Hat Media
TOOL	Macromedia FreeHand 8

337

Miscellaneous

bluehat

MEDIA •••••

DESIGN FIRM	Gardner Design
ART DIRECTOR	Chris Parks
DESIGNER	Chris Parks
CLIENT	Ares
TOOL	Macromedia FreeHand

1

cherry
pie

2

YES

YOUR ELECTRICAL SUPPLY SOURCE

3

PAWS

Play, adventure and walking services for your dog.

1 **DIGITAL SOUP** | ART DIRECTOR **PASH** | CLIENT **CHERRY PIE**
2 **WAVE 3** | DESIGNER **RHONDA HARSHFIELD**
3 **BAKKEN CREATIVE CO.** | ART DIRECTOR **MICHELLE BAKKEN** | CLIENT **PAWS**

1

2

1 **DESIGN GUYS** | ART DIRECTOR **STEVEN SIKORA** | DESIGNER **ANNE PETERSON** | CLIENT **ANDRA PATZOLDT**
2 **MORRIS CREATIVE INC.** | ART DIRECTOR **STEVEN MORRIS** | DESIGNER **DEANNE WILLIAMSON** | CLIENT **WATTERS & WATTERS**

Frank Cottrell Boyce

Archer Street

Studio 5, 10-11 Archer Street
London W1V 7HG
tel. +44 (0)20 7439 0540
fax. +44 (0)20 7437 1182
email. frank@archerstreet.com

 Archer Street

with compliments

 Archer Street

Studio 5, 10-11 Archer Street
London W1V 7HG
tel. +44 (0)20 7439 0540
fax. +44 (0)20 7437 1182
email. films@archerstreet.com

Archer Street Limited
Studio 5, 10-11 Archer Street
London W1V 7HG
tel. +44 (0)20 7439 0540
fax. +44 (0)20 7437 1182
email. films@archerstreet.com

Directors: Andy Paterson
Frank Cottrell Boyce   Anand Tucker

Company Registered No. 3537276

Registered Address:
10 Orange Street, London WC2H 7DQ

1

2

1 EMMA WILSON DESIGN CO. | DESIGNER EMMA WILSON | CLIENT EMMA WILSON DESIGN CO.
2 EMMA WILSON DESIGN CO. | DESIGNER EMMA WILSON | CLIENT EMMA WILSON DESIGN CO.

y'know
71 beak street london W1F 9SP
tel +44 (0)20 7439 4780 fax +44 (0)20 7439 4775
enquiries@yknow.com

GOLDEN BOOTS

ebdon	s.davis
	taylor
doherty	

Catwoman	The Riddler	The Joker	Penguin	Poison Ivy	Harley Quinn

sulphuric acid	battery acid	lemon juice	orange juice	coffee	tea	Doctor Destiny	Harvey Dent
Olive Oil	Spaghetti	water	milk	blood	sea water	calculator	King Tut
Baking Soda	milk of magnesia	salt	lime	Domestic Bleach	Caustic Soda		

y'know

Jolyon Gadd

71 beak street london W1F 9SP
tel +44 (0)20 7439 4780 fax +44 (0)20 7439 4775
Mobile 07775 863 792 jolyon@yknow.com

WESTERNS

...BIG NAMES

River Phoenix	Dylan Thomas	Lord Byron	Neal Cassady	Ken Kesey	Jim Morrison
			Sid Vicious	Nick Drake	Keith Moon
			Oliver Reed	DJ Screw	Charles Bukowski

y'know

y'know
71 beak street london W1F 9SP
tel +44 (0)20 7439 4780
fax +44 (0)20 7439 4775
enquiries@yknow.com

Kathy Bates	Rosie O'Donnell	Rik Waller	John Belushi	Ricki Lake	John Candy	John Goodman
Winston Churchill	Oliver Hardy	Chubby Checker	Orson Welles	Roosevelt	Maradona	Sydney Greenstreet

WHY NOT ASSOCIATES | ART DIRECTOR WHY NOT ASSOCIATES | CLIENT Y'KNOW

HOME PACKAGE DELIVERY BOX

1 **CITY OF KITCHENER** | ART DIRECTOR **JOLENE MacDONALD** | CLIENT **CIRCA DEVELOPMENT**

2 **HG DESIGN** | ART DIRECTOR **STEVE COOPER** | CLIENT **BOBBYBOX**

3 **SAYLES GRAPHIC DESIGN** | ART DIRECTOR **JOHN SAYLES** | CLIENT **MOORE FAMILY**

4 **SAYLES GRAPHIC DESIGN** | ART DIRECTOR **JOHN SAYLES** | CLIENT **SAYLES GRAPHIC DESIGN**

1

westone
PLASTIC AND COSMETIC SURGERY

2

riskcapitalpartners

3

ellisknox
PRODUCT INNOVATION

1 WILSON HARVEY | ART DIRECTOR PAUL BURGESS | DESIGNER DANIEL ELLIOTT | CLIENT WEST ONE PLASTIC SURGEONS
2 WILSON HARVEY | ART DIRECTOR PAUL BURGESS | DESIGNER DANIEL ELLIOTT | CLIENT RISK CAPITAL PARTNERS
3 WILSON HARVEY | ART DIRECTOR PAUL BURGESS | DESIGNER STEPHANIE HARRISON | CLIENT ELLIS KNOX

DESIGN FIRM	Gardner Design
ART DIRECTOR	Chris Parks
DESIGNER	Chris Parks
CLIENT	Prairie State Bank
TOOL	Macromedia FreeHand

PRAIRIE
STATE · BANK

DIRECTORY OF CONTRIBUTORS

A Plus B
New York, NY 10011, USA

A1 Design
601 Minnesota Street, #120
San Francisco, CA 94107, USA

A2- Graphics/SW/HK
42 Charlotte Road
Amsterdam, The Netherlands

AC/DC- Art Chantry Design Company
P.O. Box 4069
Seattle, WA 98104, USA

After Hours Creative
1201 East Jefferson B100
Phoenix, AZ 85034, USA

Air Design

ALR Design
2701 Edgewood Ave
Richmond, VA 23219, USA

Anderson Thomas Design
110 29th Avenue North, Suite 100
Nashville, TN 37203, USA

Arrowstreet Graphic Design
212 Elm Street
Somerville, MA 02144, USA

art + corporate culture
A-1060 Wien
Esterhazyg.19 Austria

ARTiculation Group & Benchmark
  Porter Novelli
33 Bloor Street East, Suite 1302
  M4W 3T4
Toronto, Ontario, Canada

Bailey/Franklin
0121 SW Bancroft Street
Portland, OR 97201, USA

Bakken Creative Co. Special Modern
  Design
Berkeley, CA 94704, USA

Bakker Design
4507 98th Street
Urbandale, IA 50322, USA

Balance Design
23 Almira Drive
Greenwich, CT 06830,USA

Barbara Chan Design
614 South Saint Andrews, Suite 409
Las Angeles, CA 90005, USA

Base Art Co.
The Ripley House, 623 High Street
Worthington, OH 43085, USA

Be.Design
1323 4th Street
San Rafael, CA, 94901, USA

Beaulieu Concepts Graphiques, Inc.
38 Adelaide Avenue
Candiac, Quebec J5R 3J7 Canada

Becker Design
225 East St. Paul Avenue, Suite 300
Milwaukee, WI 53202, USA

Big Eye Creative, Inc.
101-1300 Richards Street
Vancouver, BC V68 3G6 Canada

Blue I Design
Imperial House, Lypiatt Road
Cheltenham GL50 2QJ, UK

Bob's Haus
3728 McKinley Boulevard
Sacramento, CA 95816, USA

Bruce Yelaska Design
1546 Grant Avenue
San Francisco, CA 94133, USA

Buchanan Design
1035 F Street
San Diego, CA 92101, USA

Bullet Communications, Inc.
200 South Midland Avenue
Joliet, IL 60436, USA

Burd & Patterson
206 5th Street
W. Des Moines, IA 50265, USA

C.W.A., Inc.
4015 Ibis Street
San Diego, CA 92103, USA

Cahan & Associates
171 Second Street
San Francisco, CA 94102, USA

Cahoots
30 Fenway
Boston, MA, 02115, USA

Catalina Design Group
8911 Complex Drive, Suite F
San Diego,CA 92123, USA

Cato Partners
254 Swan Street
Richmond 3121 Australia

Cato Purnell Partners
10 Gipps Street
Richmond, Victoria, Austrailia

CFX Creative
1685 H Street
Bellingham, WA 98225, USA

Chase Design Group
2019 Riverside Drive
Los Angeles, CA 90027, USA

Choplogic
2014 Cherokee Parkway
Louisville, KY 40204, USA

Christopher Gorz Design
1122 Cambridge Drive
Grayslake, IL 60030, USA

cincodemayo
5 de Mayo #1058 pte.
Monterrey, NL Mexico 64000

City of Kitchener
Kitchener ON, Canada

Creative Services

Cynthia Patten

D Zone Studio
273 West 7th Street
San Pedro, CA 90731, USA

D. Design
East Peckham, Tonbridge
Kent, England

D4 Creative Group
161 Leverington Avenue, Suite 1001
Philadelphia, PA 19127-2034, USA

Design Center
15119 Minnetonka Boulevard
Mound, MN 55364, USA

Design Consultants

Design Guys
119 North Fourth Street, #400
Minneapolis, MN 55401, USA

Designstudio CAW
Krugstrasse 16
30453 Hannover, Germany

The Diecks Group
530 Broadway, 9th Floor
New York, NY 10012, USA

Digital Soup
P.O. Box 589
Culver City, CA 90030, USA

DogStar
626 54th Street South
Birmingham, AL 35203, USA

Drive Communications
133 West 19th Street
New York City, NY 10011, USA

Duarte Design
809 Costa Drive, Suite 210
Mountain View, CA 94040, USA

Duo Design
185, Rue de Paris, 94220
Charenton-le-pont, France

Dynamo Design
5 Upper Ormond Quay
Dublin, Ireland

Earthlink Creative Services
3100 New York Drive
Pasadena, CA 91107, USA

Emery Vincent Design
NSW
Surrey Hills, Sydney, Australia

Emma Wilson Design Co.
500 Aurora Avenue North
Seattle, WA 98104, USA

Energy Energy Design
246 Blossom Hill Road
Los Gatos, CA 95032, USA

Exhibit A Communications

Focus Design & Marketing Solutions
3800 Valley Light Drive
Pasadena, CA 91107, USA

Freshbrand, Inc.
Denver, CO 80202, USA

Fuel Creative
23 College Street
Greenville, SC 29601, USA

Fuszion Collaborative
901 Prince Street
Alexandria, VA 22314, USA

Gardner Design
3204 East Douglas
Wichita, KS 67208, USA

Gary Baseman
257 South Lucerne Blvd
Los Angeles, CA 90012, USA

Gasket
Paddington, Brisbane, Australia

Gee + Chung Design
38 Bryant Street, Suite 100
San Francisco, CA 94105, USA

Gillespie Design Inc.
121 East 24th St
New York, NY 10011, USA

Ginger Bee Creative
Last Chance Gulch
Helena, MT 59601, USA

Good Dog Design

Gott Folk McCann-Erikson
Reykjavic, Iceland

Gottschalk + Ash International
113 Dupont Street, M5R1V4
Reykjavic, Iceland

Gouthier Design, Inc.
P.O. Box 840925
Hollywood, FL 33084, USA

Grafik Communications, Ltd.
1199 North Fairfax Street, suite 700
Alexandria, VA 22314, USA

Graphiculture
322 1st Avenue North, #304
Minneapolis, MN 55401, USA

Graphische Formgebung
Pulverstrasse 25, 44869
Bochum, Germany

Greteman Group
142 North Mosley, 3rd Floor
Witchita, KS 67209, USA

Gunnar Swanson Design Office
536 South Catalina Street
Ventura CA 93001, USA

Gwen Francis Design Group
357 Main Street
Los Altos, CA 94022, USA

Halleck
700 Welch Road, #310
Palo Alto, CA 94304, USA

Hamagami/ Carroll & Associates
1316 3rd Street, Promenade, #305
Santa Monica, CA 90401, USA

Han/ Davis Group
2933 North Sheridan, Apt. 1417
Chicago, IL 60657, USA

Head Quarter
Frauenlobstraße 9
Mainz, Germany

Henderson Tyner Art Co.
315 N. Spruce Street, suite 299
Winston-Salem, NC 27101, USA

HG Design
1509 Briggs Street
Wichita, KS 67202, USA

Honey Design
660 Maitland Street
London, ON, Canada

Hornall Anderson Design Works, Inc.
1008 Western Avenue, Suite 600
Seattle, WA 98104, USA

Howard Levy Design

I. Paris Design
246 Gates Avenue
Brooklyn, NY 11238, USA

Icehouse Design
266 West Rock Avenue
New Haven, CT 06515, USA

Insight Design Communications
322 South Mosley
Wichita, KS 67202, USA

Iridium, A Design Agency
Ottawa, ON, Canada

Iron Design
120 North Aurora Street, Suite 5A
Ithaca, NY 14850, USA

Jane Cameron Design
276 Flinders Street
Adelaine, SA, Australia

Jay Smith Design
4709 Idaho Avenue
Nashville, TN 37209, USA

Jeff Fisher LogoMotives
P.O. Box 17155
Portland, OR 97217-0155, USA

Jim Lange Design
203 North Wabash Avenue
Chicago, IL 60601, USA

Kaiserdicken
194 Cherry Street
Burlington, VT, 05401, USA

Karacters Design Group
1600-777 Hornby,
Vancouver, BC, Canada

Karizma Culture
319 Pender Street W #310
Vancouver, BC, Canada

Kirima Design Office
5F, 1-5, Park-Bild, Yorikimachi
Yorikimachi, Kita-ku, Osaka-City,
 530-0036, Japan

Kolegram Design
Hull, QC, Canada

Korn Design
22 Follen Street
Boston, MA 02116, USA

Laughlin/ Winkler, Inc.
4 Clarendon Street
Boston, MA 02116, USA

Le- Palmier
Hamburg, Germany

Leagas Delaney SF
2nd Floor
San Francisco, CA 94105, USA

Lemley Design Co.
4735 Univ View Place Ne
Seattle, WA 98104, USA

Leo Pharmaceutical Products
Industriparken 55
Ballerup 2750 Denmark

Lewis Communications
300 Burton Hills Blvd.
Mobile, AL 36602, USA

Lewis Moberly
33 Gresse Street
London, W1P 2LP, UK

Lima Design
215 Hanover Street
Boston, MA 02113, USA

Liska + Associates
23rd Floor, 515 N. State Street
Chicago, IL 60606, USA

Lloyd's Graphic Design and
 Communication
35 Dillion Street
Belenheim, New Zealand

Louey/ Rubino Design Group
2525 Main Street, Suite 204
Santa Monica, CA, 90405, USA

Love Communications
533 South 700 East
Salt Lake City, UT 84101, USA

Lux Design
550 15th Street, #25A
San Francisco, CA 94103, USA

Marc-Antoine Hermann

Marius Farner Design
Lastropsweg 5
20255 Hamburg, Germany

McGaughy Design
3706-A Steppes Court
Falls Church, VA, 22041, USA

Melanie Sherwood
1700 Newning Avenue
Austin, TX 78704, USA

Method
972 Mission Street
San Francisco, CA 94103, USA

Metzler Associates
Charonne 75011
Paris, France

Miaso Design
Chicago, IL 60606, USA

Michael Doret Graphic Design
6545 Cahuenga Terrace
Hollywood, CA 90068, USA

Mires Design
2345 Kettner Boulevard
San Diego, CA 92101, USA

Miriello Grafico, Inc.
419 West G Street
San Diego, CA 92101, USA

Modelhart Grafik-Design DA
A-5600 St. Johann/ Pg Ing.
Ludwig Pech Str. 7, Austria

Monderer Design
2067 Massachusetts Avenue, # 3
Cambridge, MA 02138, USA

Monster Design
7826 Leary Way Ne Suite 200
Redmond, WA 98052, USA

Morris Creative Inc.
San Diego, CA 92101, USA

Murrie Lienhart Rysner
325 West Huron Street
Chicago, IL 60607, USA

Nassar Design
11 Park Street, #1
Brookline, MA 02446, USA

NB Studio
4-8 Emerson Street
London, UK

Nesnadny + Schwartz
10803 Magnolia Drive
Cleveland, OH 44106, USA

North Bank
16 Gay Street
Bath, UK

Oakley Design Studios
921 SW Morrison, Suite 540
Portland, OR 97205, USA

Oliver Russell & Associates
202 North 9th Street
Boise, ID 83702, USA

Pacey + Pacey
North Vancouver, BC, Canada

Palmquist Creative
P.O. Box 325
Bozeman, MT 59771, USA

Parachute Design
120 S. 6th Street
Minneapolis, MN 55402, USA

Patricia Bruning Design
1045 Sansome Street, Suite 219
San Francisco, CA 94111, USA

Pham Phu Design
Hohenzollernstr.97
Munich 80796 Germany

Phillips Design Group
27 Drydock Avenue
Boston, MA 02210, USA

Planet Design Company
605 Williamson Street
Madison, WI 53703, USA

Platform Creative
Seattle, WA, USA

Plum Notion Design Laboratory
140 Huyshope Avenue
Hartford, CT 06106, USA

Plus Design Inc.
25 Drydock Avenue
Boston, MA 02210, USA

PM Design
62 Robbins Avenue
Berkley Heights, NJ 07922, USA

The Point Group
5949 Sherry Lane, Suite 1800
Dallas, TX 75225, USA

Pomegranate
139 Upper Street
London, UK

Publicidad Gomez Chica
Cra. 43E No. 910
Medellin, Columbia

Punkt
58 Gansevoort Street
New York, NY, 10014, USA

Pure Design Inc.
2808 NE Martin Luther King Blvd
Portland, OR 97204, USA

PXL8R Visual Communications
P.O. Box 7678
Van Nuys, CA 91409, USA

R2 Design/ Ramalho & Rebelo, Lda.
Praceta D. Nuno Alvares Pereira, 20;5FQ
4450 218 Matosinhos, Portugal

Re: Salzman Designs
2304 East Baltimore Street
Baltimore, MD 21202, USA

Reactor Art + Design
51 Camden Street
Toronto, ON, Canada

Red Design
11 Jew Street
Brichton, United Kingdom

Refinery Design Company
2001 Alta Vista Street
Dubuque, IA 50310, USA

revoLUZion
Uhlandstr. 4
78579 Neuhausen Germany

Richards Design Group, Inc.
5616 Kingston Park
Knoxville, TN 37919, USA

Rick Johnson & Company
1120 Pennsylvania Street NE
Albuquerque, NM 87102, USA

The Riordon Design Group
131 George Street
Oakville, Ontario, L6J 3B9, Canada

RKS Design
350 Conejo Ridge Ave
Thousand Oaks, CA 91320, USA

Robert Froedge Design
Franklin, TN 37064, USA

Roslyn Eskind Associates Limited
471 Richmond Street West
Toronto, Ontario, Canada

Rubin Cordaro Design
115 North 1st Street
Minneapolis, MN 55402, USA

Russell, Inc.
119 Spadina Avenue, Level 5
Toronto, Ontario, M5V 2L1 Canada

Sagmeister Inc.
206 West 23rd Street, 4th Floor
New York, NY 10011, USA

Sametz Blackstone Associates
40 w. Newton Street
Boston, MA 02118, USA

Sayegh Design
24734 Independence Drive, #3111
Farmington, MI 48333, USA

Sayles Graphic Design
308 8th Street
Des Moines, IA 50309, USA

Scott Stern
8 Minerva Way
Glasgow G38AU

Second Floor
443 Folsom Street
San Francisco, CA 94105, USA

Segura, Inc.
1110 N. Milwaukee Avenue
Chicago, IL 60622, USA

Selbert Perkins Design Collaborative

Seltzer Design
30 The Fenway
Boston, MA 02215, USA

Shamlian Advertising
10 East Sproul Road
Springfield, PA 19064, USA

Siebert Design

Simon & Goetz Design

Slover and Company
584 Broadway, Suite 903
New York, NY 10001, USA

Sonsoles Llorens
Caspe 56
Barcelona 08010 Spain

Spin Productions
620 King Street West
Toronto, Ontario, Canada

Steven Curtis Design, Inc.
1807 West Sunnyside
Chicago, IL 60640, USA

Stewart Monderer Design, Inc.
10 Thacher Street, Suite 112
Boston, MA 02213, USA

Stoltze Design
49 Melcher Street
Boston, MA 02210, USA

Studio Bubblan
7:E Villagatan 28
50454 Boras, Sweden

Studio Hill
417 Second Street SW
Albuquerque, NM 87102, USA

Synergy Design
600 Nottingham Oaks, Suite 279
Houston, TX 77079, USA

Tharp Did It
50 University Avenue
Los Gatos, CA 95030, USA

ThinkDesign + Communications
407 N. Washington Street
Falls Church, VA 22046, USA

Tom & John: ADC
San Francisco, CA 94105, USA

Total Creative
9107 Wilshire Boulevard
Beverly Hills, CA 90210, USA

Up Design Bureau
209 East William Street, Suite 1100
Wichita, KS 67202, USA

Vanderbyl Design
171 2nd Street
San Francisco, CA 94109, USA

Vestigio, Lda.
Av. Sidonio Pais, 379
Salas 4-5 P-4100 Porto, Portugal

Visual Dialogue
429 Columbus Avenue #1
Boston, MA 02116, USA

Vrontikis Design Office
2021 Pontius Pilot Avenue
Los Angeles, CA 90025, USA

Walker Thomas Associates Melbourne
Top Floor, Osment Building
Maples Lane Prahran 3181, Australia

Wallace Church
330 East 48th Street
New York, NY 10020, USA

Warren Group
622 Hampton Drive
Venice, CA 90231, USA

Wave 3
725 South Floyd Street
Louisville, KY 40202, USA

Werk-Haus
71-3 Medan Setia 1 Bukit Damansara
50490 Kuala Lumpur, Malaysia

Why Not Associates
22C Shepherdess Walk
London, UK

Wilson Harvey
50 Poland Street
London, UK

Woodworth Associates
151 Newbury Street
Portland, ME 04101, USA

X Design Company
2525 West Main Street, #201
Littleton, CO 80120, USA

y'know

Yes Design
4401 Wilshire Blvd
Los Angeles, CA 90010, USA

ZigZag Design
4006 Oak Street #3
Kansas City, MO 64106, USA

INDEX